Greek Thinking

Demetri Lymberatos

Greek Thinking

The Art of Making Values-based, Goal-oriented
Decisions

Demetri Lymberatos

ISBN: 9798596825732

For more information, please visit
www.GreekThinking.com

Or contact:
GreekThinking@gmail.com

Dedication:

I dedicate this book to my grandma Oreanthe, whom I love very much. My grandma not only raised her children, but as a typical Greek mother, she nurtured and raised her grandchildren.

All the years that I spent with her as a baby, as a child, and as a teenager, helped me to develop. Her love and courage influenced my growth and Greek Thinking!

None of us are perfect. We should judge people on the ways that they contribute to society, and not on what others say.

My grandmother's perception on life, with all of her struggles over the course of 100 years, show us that we can be optimistic, living in gratitude.

She is always thankful and grateful for the family we have and for the opportunities we create. I'll always work to prove worthy of her love.

Table of Contents

New Journey
Chapter 1

I began writing this book shortly after I walked out of a federal detention center. My family picked me up at 500 Pearl Street, lower Manhattan's federal courthouse, known as the Southern District of New York.

It's perhaps the most famous courthouse in the nation, where federal prosecutors bring charges against business leaders and Mafia chieftains. It's hard for me to believe that authorities had locked me into the same building as where they keep notorious terrorists. In my entire life, I never imagined that I'd go into that building, or walk out of it as a defendant in a criminal case.

While we drove north to our home in Flushing, Queens, I started to map out this project in my head, knowing I had begun a new journey, one that would be completely unfamiliar to me. Every decision I made going forward would have a massive influence on the rest of my life.

I would have preferred to continue living in the same productive manner that had guided all of my earlier decisions. Within a few short years, a solid work ethic led to my starting and operating a series of neighborhood pharmacies.

Over time, I expected to grow the retail business into one that would create jobs for more people and contribute to vibrant communities. Yet from the moment I stepped foot into that federal courthouse, I knew that my life had changed. Authorities brought charges against me. As a result, I had to stand before a judge, and then I had to hire attorneys that would help me navigate the mess I had gotten myself into.

For a person who considered himself a man of the people, a law-abiding citizen, facing a felony charge could really disrupt the mindset. To use an analogy from the sea, it's as if I'd been sailing along in calm waters, but suddenly I found myself in a tempestuous storm. If I didn't respond well to the risks ahead, the storm could sink me.

The lawyers involved might drag the case out for several months, or several years. While they worked the case through judicial proceedings, I had to do something. Otherwise I would feel like a puppet, with others pulling the strings of my life.

From my perspective, all people can use this same strategy to emerge from difficult times. We have to start by accepting that we've got a problem we want to solve. We have to identify a solution, or the best possible outcome. Then we have to create a methodical plan we can follow, given the changed circumstances of our life. Then, we have to execute our plan until we get the outcome we want.

I never ask anyone to do anything that I'm not doing. And given the changed circumstances that I now find myself in, I'm writing these sentences and paragraphs as part of my plan. I'll use the plan as part of a guide to make it through the challenges ahead.

In the end, regardless of how a judge rules on my case, I understand that a day of reckoning awaits. An arrest record exists. Press reports complicate the good name I have worked so hard to build.

Like anyone else that wants to overcome a problem, I have to be ready. If I make good decisions, I can start charting my pathway to a new and better life. If I make bad decisions, I could easily sink into personal despair, blaming others and complaining of unfairness.

Each of us, as human beings, go through challenging times at various stages. Facing challenges is a part of life. Either we overcome or we perish. Some people succeed by facing struggles and difficulties with courage, confident in their ability to overcome. For others, the setbacks, or changed circumstances obliterate hope.

In fact, while writing these pages, we're all in the midst of having to cope with change. The Coronavirus has afflicted all of humanity. In the United States, more than 10 million people have contracted the virus.

The pandemic has devastated parts of the economy, raising unemployment levels to unprecedented heights and decimating entire sectors, like restaurants or leisure travel.

Schools, businesses, and events that gather people together have shut down. These changes necessitate that people reassess their choices and the values by which they live. I'm confident that I can help. I'm writing this story with hopes of showing others the pathway that I'm carving out for myself, with hopes of inspiring or teaching those who follow along with me on the journey.

With the changing world, it's becoming clearer that all of us need to think differently. Decisions that have worked for many people in the past may no longer serve people in the future. We need to consider options available. Given the changes at hand, what can we do to build fulfilling, sustainable lives?

Our Labyrinths:

It's as if we're going into a labyrinth. Each decision comes with twists and turns, opportunities and threats. We don't know what awaits us. But our survival depends upon making good choices. We can learn from the stories of others who've had to overcome struggles that threatened their existence.

In Greek mythology, we have the story of Theseus, the hero who saved his people by slaying the minotaur, a beast that had been devouring the nation's youth. The minotaur lived in hiding, deep inside of a subterranean labyrinth from which no one had ever escaped. Understanding the risks, Theseus put a plan in place. To achieve his goal, he tied one end of string to a tree, and the other end of the string to his ankle. Then he descended into the maze, confronted the beast, and killed the minotaur by stabbing it with his sword.

Unlike others who had gotten lost in the labyrinth and never made their way out, Theseus had created a plan before venturing into the darkness. He relied upon the string as a guide that would lead him back to the safety of home.

When confronting challenging times, or external threats, we all need the wisdom of Theseus. We need to plan, to create our guides that will lead us to better times. We grow stronger when our plan shows us how to go from where we are, to where we want to be. It takes us from our problem to the successful solution, as we're defining success. Once we know what we want to achieve, we can chart our course that will take us from the troubles of today, to the success of tomorrow.

I'd like to say that I learned these strategies on my own, but as a Greek American, lessons from leaders like Theseus inspired decisions I made throughout my entire life. Since childhood, I knew and understood that I wanted to open new opportunities.

I'll always give credit to lessons I've learned from the wise people who lived before me—especially my grandmother Oreanthe. She is an amazing woman whom I'll write about more in the chapters to come.

At this point, you should know that it was my grandmother and my parents that introduced me to the philosophers, the poets, the writers who told stories from which all of us can learn. Besides those great teachers, we can also look to stories from everyday people around us.

We all learn lessons along the journey of life. Some of us respond well to books, or a classroom setting. Others, like me, cannot learn while sitting at a desk in a classroom. I was too restless, eager to participate in the world rather than listen to other people who advised me how to live in the world.

The good news is that with the Internet, we don't have to sit in a classroom. At any time, we can choose to invest in ourselves and learn on our own. In this changing world, we don't need to take on hundreds of thousands of dollars in student-loan debt to get the knowledge we need to build the lives that we want to live. Ask me how I know!

As the youngest child of five, I learned the importance of speaking up early. I have three sisters and a brother; I have nieces and nephews. Family, our culture, our community has always been at the center of my life. Our parents were self-made immigrants from Greece. They taught us the importance of developing a disciplined work ethic and learning from the wisdom of people that lived before us. Now with schools being closed because of the pandemic, it's more important than ever for people to learn lessons independently, in the same way that I have learned.

My mother and father both immigrated from the world-famous and amazing islands off the shore of mainland Greece when they were teenagers.

Wanting to make their way in the land of opportunity, they left their beloved homeland with hope for a better life. They sailed to America penniless. Rather than using the traditional route of a university education, they relied upon hard work and discipline to advance. In time, they built businesses that would sustain my three sisters, my brother, and me.

Despite starting as dishwashers and cooks, hard work enabled my father to become a restaurant owner while my mother nurtured us at home. Later, my dad saw a new opportunity. He sold his restaurants to open a food warehouse that would service other neighborhood restaurant owners with daily deliveries.

With shifts that started in the late afternoon and kept him working until the early mornings, I hardly saw him when I was a young boy. Later, my father sold the warehouse to launch a new business, as the owner of a construction company. His work ethic taught me a great deal about what it means to be a good citizen.

From my parents, I learned the importance of building strong communities, of family, and of being self-reliant. When situations change, we cannot be afraid to adjust.

If we face challenges, our mindset will become our biggest asset or our biggest liability. Some people face a challenge, and they don't know how to react. Yet all of us can develop an inner strength, a confidence to change direction when we see storms on the horizon. Anyone can learn to develop this inner fortitude, but it all begins with knowing how to define success. We've got to make adjustments when situations change.

The Greeks have always had to adapt. Legends that have guided Greek thought for thousands of years inspired me. My parents and grandparents passed these stories along to me, and I listened to them intently, always striving to prove worthy of the sacrifices that others made so that I could reach a higher potential.

More than anyone, my grandmother, Oreanthe, influenced my thought. Her name translates from Greek to mean "beautiful flower," and she has always been my inspiration. As I write these words, she is 100 years old, still living independently on her island of Kefalonia, in the Ionian Sea, west of Mainland Greece.

Ithaki, the island adjacent to Kefalonia, was the home of Odysseus, the legendary figure of Homer's epic poem *The Odyssey*. In fact, when my father opened his first restaurant, he called it The Odyssey, an homage to his homeland.

The Odyssey:

With the challenges I face today, I'm reminded of Homer's story. As a great warrior, Odysseus traveled to Troy and devised a plan to penetrate the walls.

Yet fighting the battle would only be one leg on his journey. New travails would await him once he set sail through treacherous seas that separated him from home. It would take ten years, and many battles for him to make it back to his wife, Penelope, who waited for him on Ithaki.

Odysseus relied upon wisdom and courage to maintain commitment when confronting life's challenges. Instead of complaining, he battled Poseidon's son the cyclops, the sirens, the winds, and unimaginable obstacles. Despite what challenges came, he never lost sight of what he wanted to achieve. Odysseus succeeded because he chose to live in the world as it existed, rather than complaining or making excuses.

Challenges come. He could accept those challenges and live without clouding his thoughts with how he wanted things to be. As I learned from my 100-year old grandmother, Odysseus lived with the virtue of persistence.

I grew up listening and learning from Greek mythology and philosophy. Although not a good student in school, I learned a great deal about being self-directed from the stories of my heritage.

Leaders like Socrates, Plato, Aristotle, and Epictetus taught that philosophy was not a theoretical, academic discipline. Rather, philosophy was a way of life, a way of thinking and adjusting in a changing world. We cannot allow ourselves to get drunk with happiness when times are good; nor can we allow ourselves to sink into despair when times are bad. We simply have to adjust, evenly, with calm minds, confident that we can adjust to changing situations.

Events that are beyond our control take place in the world. We must accept the good times with the bad times, always striving to focus on what we can control—developing our mindset and discipline. From leaders who lived before us, or stories that others have written about, we learn that how we think and how we act influences what we become.

Earlier decisions have taken me into unexpected storms. They're beyond my ability to control. But like all of the great leaders from whom I have learned, I know that I have the power within to adjust. To succeed, I must define the best possible outcome, given the strengths and weaknesses of my life. Now is not the time for me to lose sight of what I want to become. Rather, it's the time to reflect. While lawyers work my case through the judicial system, I will not sit by idly, waiting for the outcome. Instead, I'll use this time to lay out my plan, writing out lessons I've learned and charting out the next course of action that I will take.

Introspection:

As a 34-year-old man who barely finished high school, I know that writing will not be easy. Yet no one ever succeeded by trying the easy route.

We've got to identify where we are, figure out where we want to go, and then lay out the course that will help us become what we're setting out to become.

For some of us, that path may include graduating from high school, going on to college, and then starting out a career that goes precisely as planned. In this era of the pandemic, however, all of us should know that regardless of what plans we make—life may change. When life changes, we've got to be willing to recalibrate and prepare to rebuild—just as I'm doing now. As Socrates taught us, "the unexamined life is not worth living."

My birth name is Dimitrios Lymberatos. As a young boy, becoming more Americanized, I changed my name to Demetri. It's what I go by now. The name was too long for other students to say when I was going through school.

As my life has changed, I've turned to the wisdom of Socrates for a reason. Some of you may know his story. As a man of wisdom, he lived in Athens of ancient Greece, more than 2,500 years ago.

During that class-based society, laws prohibited people who were born into the ruling class from educating people who were born into the lower classes. Socrates, being a man of principle, believed that every human being had value. Rather than separating people, he believed that we could build stronger communities by spreading wisdom to all. Despite the laws that existed, Socrates chose to teach, and he taught thousands of people, regardless of their class or status.

In fact, he taught so much that his wisdom has lived with us for thousands of years, thanks to the writings of his student, Plato, and then Plato's student, Aristotle. Plato wrote *The Republic*, to compile all of the lessons he learned from Socrates.

While going through my own travails, I turned to those stories again. I wanted to refamiliarize myself with the story of Socrates, because in some ways, I felt aligned with him. The story of his time in a jail cell inspired me to want to do better.

Authorities had arrested Socrates, charging that he had violated the law by teaching slaves how to read and how to think differently. After a trial, the judges convicted Socrates and sentenced him to death. While Socrates waited for the day of his execution, he received a visit in the jail from his friend, Crito.

Crito came bearing good news. He told Socrates that friends and admirers volunteered to offer him support. They agreed to bribe the jailer who would open the gates and provide additional resources to sustain Socrates so that he could live out the remaining years of his life in exile.

After listening to Crito's generous offer, Socrates declined. When Crito asked why he would remain in jail when the sentence would mean certain death, Socrates gave his answer, which I paraphrase below:

We live in a democracy. In a democracy, we have to take the good with the bad. Athens has clothed me and fed me. It has educated me and protected me from foreign enemies. I have taken all of the good. I must also take the bad. And this is a bad law. But in a democracy, we have the right to work toward changing laws if we don't agree with those laws. We do not have the right to break laws.

It is a bad law that prohibits us from serving the people. Yet since I broke the law, I will pay the price for the bad decision I made. I will not run away like a coward from a problem that my own decisions created.

Like Socrates, I did not want to run away from problems I created.

My lawyers will work through the judicial system, but the responsibility will be mine to adjust. Regardless of what happens to me going forward, I have a duty and a responsibility to make things right with my community.

At this stage, it's understandable that readers may want to know what challenges I faced with the law. Just as the Ancient Greeks taught us the virtue of persistence, they also taught us the virtue of patience. In due time, I'll reveal decisions I made that necessitated me to change course—all good things come to those who wait.

The more salient message is that, like Socrates, I've tried to live as a man of the people, and a man of principle. I've wanted to make decisions that would be for the good of our community.

Earlier, in this chapter, I wrote that my grandmother, Oreanthe, has lived on the island of Kefalonia for 100 years. My mother's family hailed from Kos, another one of the Greek islands in the Aegean Sea.

Like Kefalonia influenced me with its proximity to Odysseus's island of Ithaki, Kos influenced me. It is the ancestral home of Hippocrates, widely known as the father of modern medicine; his lessons taught doctors to begin with a commitment to "first, do no harm."

Despite not advancing my formal education beyond a high school diploma, the disciplined work ethic that I developed in adolescence led me into the field of healing. In the chapters ahead, I'll reveal precisely how early decisions led to my starting a business of owning neighborhood pharmacies.

Besides learning through this story of my personal odyssey from high school to pharmacy owner to felon, to recalibrating my life, I'm developing an online course.

Through that course, I'll teach those who want to learn how they too can own a pharmacy—even if they don't have a pharmacy degree. If they don't want to own a pharmacy, then they can learn lessons from the courses I create to build a different kind of business, or to become an entrepreneur, or just to reach a higher potential by learning to think like a Greek!

If you want to learn more about the courses I create, visit my website at GreekThinking.com.

Although I'll reveal these lessons from what I've learned along the journey, this book is more than about my life or what I've learned along the pathway to building a career as a self-directed entrepreneur.

Through these ten chapters, I'll map out how leaders taught me to think differently. Rather than making decisions in accordance with what others expect from us, leaders have taught that if we want to reach our highest potential, we must train our minds to define success—not success as others live it.

We have to define success for ourselves. Once we set out on that path, and we can see with clarity where we're striving to achieve, we will develop the strength to keep moving through the storms of life. And if unexpected winds start to blow us off course, we can readjust our sails, just as Homer taught us with his story of Odysseus's journey. We can make changes in ways that will take us through the storms and into safe harbors, or the next adventures in our life.

As you will see through these chapters to follow, success for me has not been about accumulating millions of dollars or living a life of luxury.

Like my grandmother, my parents, and the leaders from whom I've learned, I'm a man of the people, a believer in family and culture and community. Success, for me, will always be in bringing others together and sharing lessons that I have learned. In these changing times, where so much division exists, we all can grow stronger if we look to our future and what we want to become. That vision can carry us through the storms of today.

Through this book and through the accompanying personal-development courses I create, you will see that I never ask anyone to do anything that I'm not doing. For that reason, I'll challenge you to work alongside me.

» Start by defining success.

» What does success look like to you?

Goals and Being Deliberate
Chapter 2

In the previous chapter, I promised that I would never ask anyone to do anything that I'm not doing. We're all on our own odyssey, traveling through the storms of our life. Yet in order to get through the challenges, as we learned from the story of Theseus and his quest to kill the minotaur in the labyrinth, we need a plan.

Our plan must be intentional, something that we carved out in a deliberate way. Once we identify our plan, and document our plan, we can lay out the tiny steps we need to take along the way.

As a young boy, I learned this wisdom from my beloved grandmother. As an immigrant family with five children, we did not have a great deal of resources. My father worked hard every day to sustain us. Our parents brought us to Greece regularly; basically, we traveled to Greece every summer. The bedrock of my education came from lessons I learned while on those family excursions, and the time I spent with my grandmother on the island of Kefalonia.

Neither my grandmother, nor anyone in my family, had a proper education, as distinguished with university degrees that hung on the wall. We learned from practical lessons, handed down from the Greeks who lived before us.

From the Stoics, we learned that regardless of where we are, or what we're going through, we can invest in ourselves and strive for self-improvement. We can always change the way we think and strive to improve our lot in life if we choose to advance in slow, methodical ways.

To grow stronger, we needed good habits. Epictetus, a former Greek slave who became one of the Stoic philosophers helped us to understand that we must carve out our own lives rather than complain about hardship, or what others expect from us. Regardless of where we begin, or what changes the world brings, we're responsible for how we act and respond. For this reason, we must constantly assess our decisions and renew our commitment to self-discipline.

In the United States, where we have so much abundance, it's harder to grasp this lesson on the importance of self-discipline. While I spent time with my grandmother in Greece, I saw the real-life application of Stoic philosophy.

My grandmother grew up in a rural village, working the land or feeding the donkeys. I can only imagine the hardship that existed when she was a child, back in the early 1900s. When she became of age, my grandmother's parents arranged for her to marry my paternal grandfather; he died when I was only an infant, so I never knew him. While he was away at sea, earning a living as a deckhand on ships that traveled the world, my grandmother would stay home to rear their five children. To survive, she learned to live in gratitude for the blessings she had; it never occurred to her that she should complain about what she didn't have.

Since her parents had chosen the man she would marry, I remember asking whether she loved my grandfather. She couldn't really say whether she loved him, she said, because she hardly knew him.

They would have a child together, then he would go out to sea and stay at work for months or sometimes years at a time. When he came back into port, they would have another child, then he would return to sea, sending his paychecks home to support the family. She respected him immensely, she said, but didn't know whether love was the right word to describe their marriage.

In my eyes, my grandmother lived as a portrait of Stoic discipline. Through her actions, I learned the importance of living in gratitude, appreciative of the blessings we have. As an example of the lessons she taught, I remember the simple act of bathing.

Her home didn't have a water heater. To bathe in warm water, she taught that we had to plan and prepare. In the morning, we'd draw water from a well to fill a bucket. By leaving the bucket in the sun all day, we'd have warm water we could use to wash ourselves in the evening.

Life was about making good habits, about understanding our environment, then planning and conserving to get the highest and best use from the resources available to us. When drinking orange juice, for example, she encouraged us to pour only half of a glass to minimize waste.

Life required us to look ahead, and to take small steps that would help us make it through the hours of the day, the days of the week, the weeks of the month, and the months of the year. To think that she had been living as a portrait of discipline for a century both inspired and amazed me.

Learning and Observing:

My parents lived by that identical invest-in-thyself philosophy of the Stoics. They met by happenstance when they were both teenagers. She was selling raffle tickets at a dance. As soon as she encountered my father, he was smitten by her beauty. He kept pursuing her, eventually presenting himself at her home.

After going through the family introductions, her parents allowed my mom to begin dating my dad. At a young age, they made a commitment to each other.

Others in the community took notice of my father's disciplined work ethic. In time, he relied upon a network of relationships he built to raise the resources necessary to operate his own restaurant.

As a young man, my father worked hard, developing business lessons along the way. He operated several restaurants before transitioning into a more wholesale, service-oriented business.

By renting a warehouse, he could store food for other neighborhood restaurants. Every day, he and his team would deliver the vegetables, the milk, the cheese, the meats from his warehouse to the local restaurants. The job meant we hardly saw him.

He worked from late afternoon until the early morning hours. Since his father had supported his family by going out to sea for months at a time, my father appreciated the opportunity to sleep at home.

From my dad, I could develop an appreciation for taking little steps to improve our livelihoods. As a result of the sacrifices that my dad's parents made, he got opportunities that my grandparents did not have. And as a result of the sacrifices my parents made, opportunities opened for me that neither my mom nor my dad had.

When I was a child, I'd spend some time with him at the warehouse. The warehouse was located in a bad neighborhood of Hunts Point, in the Bronx. There was a lot of street crime in the area, with prostitution and drugs. I remember his unorthodox way of teaching.

When I was still young, perhaps six or seven, I remember working at my dad's warehouse. He asked a homeless drug addict on the street to speak with me, to tell me about the decisions that led to his life of hardship.

The man showed me drugs and told me to make sure that I never used them. I walked away from that conversation with a good understanding that if I wanted to make something of my life, I would have to carve out my way with good habits—and avoid the bad habits that could lead me down a dark and perilous path.

As a student, I studied in public schools, but I never responded well to the classroom. As the youngest child in a large family, I learned that if I wanted anyone to notice me, I had to speak up.

I couldn't make the adjustment that teachers required of students in school. They expected us to sit quietly, to listen and learn. I went through the motions to advance through elementary school at PS 32 and junior high at IS 25.

I began high school at Francis Lewis, but by the time I turned 16, my teachers said that I had fallen too far behind. Rather than allowing me to continue my education in a traditional high school, the administrators transferred me to the night school program at Flushing High School. It scared me to death.

In the night school program, I was only 16 but I had to attend classes with people that were going through some type of diversionary program to stay out of jail.

All of the other students were much older, some in their early 20s. We had to go through metal detectors when we walked through hallways, and armed security officers sat in the classrooms with us. My father explained to me that if I didn't pay attention in school, opportunities wouldn't open for me in life.

After a few quarters, the administrators deemed my progress sufficient to transfer back to a traditional school. I finished my high school years at the Whitestone Academy, the first male in my family to earn a high school diploma.

Although I wanted to make my parents proud by earning that diploma, I knew that a formal education wasn't going to be the pathway that I would choose.

Appreciation for Work:

During my junior high school years, a close friend impressed me when she told me that she had gotten a job at McDonald's. We were only 13 years old, yet through working my friend earned a paycheck that she could use as she deemed fit. I craved that independence.

When she told me that McDonald's wanted to hire more students, I went to apply. The manager gave me the job, provided I could get the school to sign off on the working papers I would need. My school authorized me to work 25 hours each week, with limitations on how late I could work on school nights.

For $5.15 per hour, I would do anything my supervisor asked. I swept the parking lot, cleaned the bathrooms, scrubbed the grill, and cleaned the fryer. Regardless of the task, I applied myself completely, wanting to prove worthy as a good employee. Each time I got a paycheck, I deposited the check into a savings account I opened. I loved going to work and I felt so grateful to build that independence. By purchasing my first pair of jeans for $90, I got a real appreciation for how hard I had to work in order to get the things that I wanted.

With my parents' permission, I could open a savings account in a bank that was adjacent to the restaurant. They gave me a passbook. Each time I got a paycheck, I would take it to the bank and begin building my account. Although I wasn't driven by money,

I loved to watch the account grow, to know that I was sowing seeds to build a better future.

After about two years of working as many hours as possible on the McDonald's job, my cousin opened a new opportunity. He was 19, and for several years he had been working at Argos Drugs, a local pharmacy in the neighborhood. My cousin had found a new job in construction, and he told me that if I wanted, I could take his position at Argos. I didn't know much about what he did, but when my cousin said that the job paid $9 hour per hour, I considered it a huge step up from what I had been doing at McDonald's. Simple math allowed me to project how much faster I'd be able to accelerate my savings plan by taking the job at Argos.

McDonald's had trained me well on the importance of punctuality, cleanliness, and having a welcoming, or friendly demeanor with customers. I learned what it meant to be a good employee. Those traits positioned me well when I switched to begin the job at Argos Drugs. By then I was 15, and I believe that the owner, Mr. Drakis, had a favorable impression of me.

While I advanced through high school, Mr. Drakis gave me increasingly higher levels of responsibility. Although I started out by cleaning the store and stocking shelves, in time he began to trust me with working the cash register and interacting more closely with customers, including doing personal deliveries. I appreciated the opportunity to work in his store.

I admired Mr. Drakis, a trained and licensed pharmacist. Many members of his family worked in the medical profession, as doctors or pharmacists. They had immigrated to America from the mainland of Greece; as evidenced by their professions, they made a commitment to formal education and training—which I admired, even though I understood that school would not be the path for me. Still I learned a great deal by observing his work ethic and wisdom.

Habits and Goals:

As I advanced from 15 to 16, I started to think about what I wanted. Like most kids that age, I wanted to own my own car. By working as many hours as possible, and being disciplined about my savings plan, I could see that my goal would be within reach.

Many kids my age would talk about wanting to get a car, but few laid out a methodical plan that would transform their dreams into a realistic pursuit. Whether a person is 15 or 51, I'm convinced that we all can use goals as a tool to help us move in the right direction. We simply have to start by asking some good questions:

» What is it that you're trying to achieve?

» In what ways will success as you define it change or influence your life?

» What are you doing today to show your commitment to succeeding with your goals?

If you know the direction you want to take, then you can use the technique of setting SMART goals to make deliberate progress. Although I didn't use the name "SMART goal," I've been using this technique since I was a teenager.

What's a SMART goal?

SMART is an acronym that helps us determine whether we're setting goals that align with what we say is important to us.

» S = Specific—Is the goal specific?

» M = Measurable—Can we measure whether we're making progress toward completion of the goal?

» A = Action-oriented—Are we setting goals that are within our reach, given our current strengths and weaknesses?

» R = Realistic—Are we setting goals that have some basis in reality?

» T = Time-bound—Do the goals we're setting out to achieve have a clear timeline, showing that we either succeeded or we failed?

I set a goal of buying my first car by the time I was 17. Because I clarified the goal, I could set measurable progress with every hour that I worked on the job. I had to use this technique in many areas of my life during those years.

For example, I still remember how my stomach used to turn in disgust when I learned that administrators were transferring me to the night-school program at Flushing. Yet I knew there wouldn't be any sense in complaining.

When I started out in high school, I valued the work that I was doing at Argos Drugs more than I valued the schoolwork. As a result, I fell behind with my classes. And as a result of falling behind in my classes, administrators transferred me to a program that I didn't like.

My father made it pretty clear to me. If I wanted to succeed in life, I had to plant seeds. There is an old saying about planting. I don't know where I heard it before, but it starts with a question about the best time to plant an oak tree. The answer, of course, is that the best time to plant an oak tree is 20 years ago. The second-best time is today.

We all make decisions today that govern what we become in the days, weeks, months, years, and decades ahead. As a 15-year old high school student, decisions I made to focus on my job at Argos meant that I fell behind in school. By falling behind in school, administrators made the decision to transfer me to the night school program at Flushing.

Complaining about it wouldn't do any good. Instead, I set a specific goal. Within two quarters, I would work and study hard and accumulate all of the extra credit assignments possible to pick up my grades. By picking up my grades, I built the credibility I needed to persuade administrators to transfer me back to a traditional school, at Whitestone Academy.

That challenge taught me that I could succeed if I:

» Set the specific goal of going back to a traditional high school,

» Measure the amount of extra credit assignments I had to complete,

» Act in accordance with the plan that I laid out,

» Realistically apply my efforts, and set

» Timelines I could keep.

That same technique allowed me to achieve a second goal that I valued during my teenage years—to buy my first car.

At that age, I didn't know anything about automobiles. Yet I believed that if I owned a car, I would have a higher level of independence. A car would bring me one step closer to feeling as if I were an adult. By the time my father was 13, he had already sailed away from his island of Kefalonia in the Ionian Sea.

He made his way across the Atlantic, went through the Panama Canal, landed in San Francisco, and made his way to New York so that he could start a family in America. If he could achieve his goals, I had every reason to believe that I could purchase a car.

With that clear goal in mind, I started to read classified ads in the newspaper. By working all the hours that I was allowed to work, and saving most of my paychecks each week, by the time I turned 17 I built my savings account to more than $1,400.

After seeing an ad that a seller placed for a 1992 Toyota Corolla, I agreed to give him the $800 purchase price and paid for the car in cash. By myself, I went to the Department of Motor Vehicles to register the car, and I signed up for my own insurance policy.

The car wasn't going to win any awards. With a bad exhaust system, the car was so loud that it triggered alarm systems whenever I turned it on. To get into the car, I had to jimmy the door open with a screwdriver. Despite those flaws, I owned the car free-and-clear, and I derived a sense of accomplishment in completing another goal.

Reflections:

As I reflect on those early years of my life, I can see how lessons from those summer months I spent with my grandmother influenced my development through life.

A disciplined and deliberate path led our family through incremental stages of growth. We went from rural villages on Greek islands, to make our home in one of the busiest cities in the world. We could start with very little, but with discipline, good habits, strong values, and commitment to family and community, we could create a life of meaning and fulfillment.

When challenges come, we simply must look ahead. If we can define success, we can set a series of deliberate goals that will bring us closer to what we want to achieve.

That disciplined path carried my grandmother through 100 years. It empowered my parents to raise a family of five children and to become honorable business owners. By learning from them, I made it through the challenges of adolescence, continuing a journey that launched my own career.

In times of struggle, we can always regroup, recalibrate, and lay out our plan for the next stage of the journey.

In what ways are you setting deliberate goals to advance along the odyssey of your life?

If you want begin Greek Thinking, remember the steps to success:

- » Step 1: Define Success,

- » Step 2: Set clear and deliberate goals.

In the next chapter, we'll talk about the importance of commitment.

Commitment: Staying True to Our Beliefs
Chapter 3

The first two chapters of this story reveal what leaders taught me about the framework for success. Basically, I understood that a two-step process would advance possibilities to make it to the other side of any challenge:

» Step 1)

◊ For a person to achieve anything in life, the person must identify success. A person must know what he or she wants to achieve;

» Step 2)

◊ After the person identifies success, the person must lay out the clearly defined, incremental goals that he or she has to achieve along the way.

These rules apply to every person, during every era. We may not be able to control when we're born, or what challenges we face. But we can always control how we're going to respond to the challenges around us.

We can always choose what success will mean to us; then we can lay out clear plans or goals that will take us from today's challenges to the better times ahead. Every day, we should reassess where we are and recommit to the success we're striving to build.

The influences in my life made these principles clear to me. I got this message by listening to the troubles of my grandmother's life.

Despite experiencing true hardship and loss, she refused to allow her traumas to influence her attitude or outlook on life. Instead, my beloved grandmother always lived productively, feeling optimistic, grateful, appreciative for what she had around her.

A Hollywood movie, *Captain Corelli's Mandolin* dramatized some of the hardships that she had to live through.

During World War II, the Italians and the Germans occupied the island of Kefalonia, where she has lived for her entire life. When she was in her early 20s, all of the men in the village had to fight against the occupiers of the island. People went out to fight and they never returned.

Our family's place on the island was on the top of a mountain, a strategically important location to all factions of the war.

The Germans and Italians had placed satellites on top of the mountain to assist with their communications. Wanting to gain advantage by disrupting Hitler's ability to communicate, the Americans and the British constantly bombed the area, destroying the infrastructure and killing countless people. The turmoil of war led to lasting destruction, meaning that for many years, my grandmother had to live without running water, without electricity, without so much that we took for granted. Yet she never complained.

All of the people from the village joined together to resist the Germans and Italian invaders.

Sadly, either the Germans or the Italians killed everyone on my grandmother's side of the family. She lost her father, her uncles, and many people who had been close to her.

They went away and never returned. Despite all of that loss, my grandmother always expressed gratitude, knowing that there would be things beyond her ability to control. Still, she could choose to live a happy life that is filled with optimism.

As a small child, when I went to stay with her, she would take me to visit the grave of my grandfather. She would go with our Greek traditions, lighting a candle to commemorate his life. She would take flowers from the nearby gardens and together we would plant them on his grave.

When I asked my grandmother when we could visit the cemetery or grave where her family members were buried, her answer made me sad. She told me that all of her family members lost their lives during the invasion of our island.

Since no one ever found the bodies, those people did not receive a proper burial, or even a grave site. Despite such struggles, my grandmother always had the strength to move forward and to live in happiness. She never faulted anyone, but always wanted to live as a great role model for us. For that reason, I love and respect her so much.

Listening to her made a lasting impression on how I saw the world. Success, for my grandmother, meant living in peace, with a positive attitude, regardless of what went on around her. With her attitude, every day was a blessing and we should never grow attached to anything other than our relationship to family, community, and God.

My father, on the other hand, wanted to pursue opportunities that were not available on his small island. As a teenager, he took the incremental steps necessary to build a new life in America.

Although he came without much in the way of financial resources, by pursuing small goals, he made his way, building opportunities to not only sustain his family, but also to provide jobs for other people to sustain their families.

I learned best from people that lived in accordance with the Stoic's philosophy. Like Epictetus, a man who came from poverty, they understood that success in life came from making a commitment to the principles by which we live; success did not mean clinging to things that others could take away from us.

As an adolescent, I could live in accordance with those same principles. I could identify success, and I could set small goals that would help me along the way. For example, knowing that I wanted independence, I pursued a job with McDonald's. By applying myself, I learned how to bring value to my employer.

By opening a savings account, I could watch those savings grow. This path led to my independence, even allowing me to make a large purchase, like my first car.

Similarly, if I faced problems, or challenges, like being transferred to a night school where I did not fit in, I could change direction. Knowing that I wanted to get back to a normal school, I set the series of small goals that would lead to success, as I defined success at that stage in my life.

If we embrace this two-step principle as a habit, and we practice that habit every day, we can achieve more than others expect from us. As I reflect on my life, I see this to be an essential point.

As I learned from the leaders around me, to truly benefit from our habits, we must practice those habits every day. We practice by asking questions of ourselves. It is a way of the Stoic philosophers. We learn by asking good questions. At any time, we can ask:

» In what way are the decisions I'm making today consistent with what I have defined as success?

Look at the power of that question. If we ask such questions of ourselves every day, we're strengthening our resolve to make better decisions.

On the other hand, if we do not know how to define success for our life, we don't have any basis to set clear goals.

There is a famous children's book, *Alice in Wonderland,* that makes this point with a character, the Cheshire Cat, which says, "If you don't know where you're going, any road will take you there."

We always have to know where we're going. And we always should be assessing ourselves, checking to make sure that we're making decisions that harmonize with what we say is important to us.

Success, in my mind, means knowing where we're going. Then it requires us to lay out the road map, the plan, the specific goals that we're going to achieve along the way.

If we adhere to that habit, and check ourselves daily, we're able to get what we want. We're able to open new opportunities that others may have thought were beyond our reach. Once we know what we want, and we identify the goals, we simply must make a commitment—a 100% commitment. Socratic questioning can become a useful technique to help us along the path.

Socratic Questioning:

In Plato's book, *The Republic*, we learn the power of introspection and questioning. By reflecting on the choices we've made, and questioning whether we made the right choices, we stay on the course of personal development.

Socrates showed us that we can grow stronger when we become more intentional. We need to consider the options that exist for us, or we should contemplate what we could do differently. By practicing this habit of Socratic questioning, we put ourselves in a better position to reach our highest potential.

We develop habits by doing the same thing day after day. We can choose to develop good habits, or bad habits. People who succeed develop good habits. But good habits in one area of life do not always translate into good habits in other areas.

For example, we all know the stories of famous people who developed incredible talents in one area but failed miserably in other areas.

Some people practice habits every day that make them world-class athletes. Some artists practice habits that make them exceptional singers or actors.

Yet becoming a successful athlete, singer, or actor does not mean a person cannot fail in other areas. A person may be great at a craft, but a person may not be able to control an addiction, or a person may not be able to control a temper.

Those flaws can lead to catastrophe, as in the case of the famous football player, Aaron Hernandez. Aaron became a professional athlete, which required a devotion to his craft. But his personal life was a mess, as evidenced by his murder conviction. Later, I read that Aaron hung himself in a prison cell.

Stories like Aaron Hernandez reaffirmed my commitment to Stoic principles. He lacked the strength of commitment to live with the problems that his own decisions created.

In contrast, my grandmother had the strength to find happiness even though she had to live through enormous struggles. It may be hard to believe, but my 100-year-old grandmother had more strength than an NFL superstar.

Likewise, my father had the strength to assess what he wanted in life, and to chart out a course that would lead to success. People who succeed renew their commitment to principles every day. They do not live for the opinions of others. Instead, they live as if they're the captains of their own ship.

As human beings, we need to assess our decisions every day, knowing that we're living a full life. We should always strive to define success in ways that make us a whole person. It doesn't do us any good to be the best in the world at one thing, if our failure in other areas leads to our demise.

Socratic questioning can help us to assess the choices we're making. The more thought we give to defining success, the more closely we can examine our habits.

» Do our habits relate to who or what we want to become?

We have to follow a principled path if we truly want to achieve what we say is important to us. To stay the course, we must exercise or practice the habits of success; we must commit to the path we have laid out to succeed. Socratic questioning becomes a useful tool that we can use to stay on course.

Although we may say that we know the path to success, if we don't strengthen our will and commit, we can easily fall off course.

By setting clear goals every day, and then using Socratic questioning techniques to gauge whether our goals align with how we've defined success, we are practicing good habits. If we do not, we can easily get off the path that we've laid out to lead us where we want to go.

In a movie, The Matrix, I heard a line that has always stayed with me.

The character Morpheus tells Neo that there is a difference between knowing the path and walking the path.

His guidance is very much like the teaching of Greek philosophers that shaped my life. Leaders remind us that a way of thinking means nothing if we're not willing to practice the habit of bringing those thoughts into our daily decisions.

With Socratic questioning, we're always assessing. We're questioning whether the decisions we're making today align with what we want to become in the months, years, or decades ahead. By asking good questions, we force ourselves to think. We should think about whether the path we've set for our life is still the right path. Sometimes, we need to adjust. We do so with questions, such as:

» In what way did the decisions I made yesterday lead me closer to my goal?

» What new opportunities will open because of the progress I made last week?

» What opportunities did I miss because of the choices I made?

Notice that the question doesn't have a right answer or a wrong answer. Socratic questions force us to think. Our responses help us assess whether the choices we're making align with how we've defined success. If we're getting closer to our goals, we're making good decisions. If we're making decisions that limit our prospects for success, we use our discretion to adjust.

Veering Off Course:

As I continue this exercise of reflecting, I see how living in accordance with this principled path guided my decisions through high school. Then, soon after I graduated, I drifted off course. Reflecting on that time of my life, I'm reminded again about *The*

Odyssey, and the adventures Homer described in his great story. We may be moving along well, but the winds can change at any time. We may not control external events, but we can always choose how we're going to respond.

By working hard and saving money since my early teens, I accumulated resources that gave me a modicum of liberty. When I told my parents that I wanted to travel and see different parts of the country, they encouraged me to find my way. While still in high school, two friends of mine joined me on a trip to California.

Like everyone else, we saw California through television shows that glamorized San Francisco and Los Angeles. While visiting San Francisco and Los Angeles, I felt alive, but I also burned through a big portion of my savings.

In retrospect, life is about going through different experiences that make us learn and grow. When I graduated from high school, I accepted a job with another pharmacy, where I worked for about a year.

Other people that had gone to high school with me were going away to college and talking about all the fun they were having. College would never be a part of my life, but I still wanted to join the good times I heard about from people I knew.

In a misguided pursuit of good times, I made the impetuous decision to move to South Florida—a place I'd never been and a place that I didn't know anything about.

Other people told me that South Florida would be an awesome place to build my life. Since I had experience of working in pharmacies, I reasoned that I could easily set up my life down there. I made the move, chasing a foolish path that, without direction, would lead to nowhere.

To use an analogy from Homer's book, Florida was about as alluring to me as the Sirens were to Odysseus.

In Greek mythology, the Sirens were a group of monsters living on an island; they survived by luring sailors from the sea to their shores, where the Sirens would devour the men. To lure the men, the monsters could transform themselves into beautiful women with exquisite voices. When the Sirens sang, the beauty of their voices lured the men to shore, and the sailors never returned.

Knowing that no sailor would be immune to the call of the Sirens, Odysseus ordered his crew members to fill their ears with beeswax so they would not be tempted to go to the island's shore.

He wanted to hear the beauty of the voices, but he did not want to succumb to the temptation of the Sirens. Since he did not fill his ears with wax, Odysseus protected himself by having his men tie him to the mast of his ship so that he could not break free; he ordered his men not to untie him until after they had sailed past the island.

He would not waver from his commitment to make it back home.

On my own odyssey, Florida called to me like the Sirens. Young and eager to join the party scene, I shifted my focus from productivity to having a good time. That directionless shift led me to lose the disciplined path I'd been on earlier; it worked out about as well as a wiser person would expect. At 19 years of age, the fast life of nightclubs and good times attracted me.

Within a few months, I burned through all of the savings that I had accumulated over the previous four years. I couldn't seem to find stability. Rather than getting ahead with a solid savings plan, I began living off my credit cards, going into debt for the first time.

After about 18 months of irresponsibility, I came to my senses. With renewed commitment, I made my way back to New York, eager to get back on the track of success.

Recalibrating:

In the previous chapter, where I wrote about the importance of setting specific, measurable, action-oriented, realistic, time-bound goals, I used an analogy of an oak tree. We know the best time to plant an oak tree is 20 years ago, but the second-best time is today. At any time, we can choose to plant a seed that will help us build a better future.

Yet planting a seed isn't quite enough. We've also got to nurture the soil around the seed, and feed the seed with nutrients, like fertilizer. The seed matures and grows through the fertilizer into a strong tree.

Many people consider the best fertilizer to be livestock manure. In other words, before a seed can grow into a strong tree, the seed must *grow through a lot of shit or "skata," as we say in Greek!*

Like the seed that aspires to grow into a strong tree, once I returned to New York from my Florida excursion, I had to grow through a lot of shit.

With more than $20,000 in credit-card debt that I didn't have a means to pay, my credit score began to fall like a brick. I didn't have sufficient credit to get a cellphone plan. Debt collectors harassed me daily.

Socrates, a man of principle, taught me that if I wanted to get through troubles, I had to face problems with dignity.

It didn't make sense for Socrates to run away from his problems, so he chose to sit in jail until authorities executed him.

I would have to take my own punishment for the bad decisions I made. When debt collectors called me on the phone, I made a commitment to make things right. I wouldn't run away from problems created by my own recklessness.

Any of us, at any time, can lose our way. With the principled path that the Stoic's teach, and the discipline of Socratic questioning, however, we can choose to reassess what we're doing at any time.

We can choose to make a different decision. To change the direction
we're going, we must simply revert to
that same, two-part strategy outlined
at the start of this chapter:

» Step 1)

◊ For a person to achieve
anything in life, the person
must identify success. A
person must know what he
or she wants to achieve;

» Step 2)

◊ After the person identifies
success, the person must
lay out the clearly defined,
incremental goals that he or
she has to achieve along the
way.

My trip to South Florida may
have taken me off track. Yet I do not
regret the experience. By going into
debt, and by facing the problems that
I created, I learned invaluable lessons
that shaped the rest of my life. Those

lessons convinced me that in order to reach our highest potential:

- » We have to define success,

- » We have to set clear goals, and

- » We have to make a 100% commitment to achieve what we say is important to achieve.

Socratic questioning will always help us to get back on track. It's all part of the journey we're on; it's the odyssey of our life.

It's the path I'm going through now, as I prepare for another storm in my life—a storm that could potentially take my liberty. If it does, count on me to move forward with my dignity intact. I am Stoic—and I believe in Greek Thinking! Shouldn't you?

In what ways have you found the concept of commitment important to your life?

Dreams and Pressures
Chapter 4

Each of us, I think, grows up with a combination of dreams and pressures. For some, problems get in the way.

They can block people from moving forward. People may aspire to build a more fulfilling life, yet if they're in the midst of struggles, or difficult circumstances, and they don't have the right mindset, they can easily lose hope.

With too much pressure, it's hard for people to see their way through to the other side, a time when they can enjoy a better life.

I'm in the midst of my own pressures now—which I'll reveal more about later. To make it through, I rely upon a strategy. I turn to the role models, mentors, and people that inspire me. They help me keep pushing forward along the journey. By now you know of my connection to Odysseus, but I also have the story of my parents—modern day Greeks that overcame enormous pressures to achieve their dreams.

We all can look to the people who brought us into the world. Or we can build strength from looking to inspiring stories of other people we admire.

On September 21, 1970, my father was a 13-year-old boy in Greece, dreaming of a better life abroad. As a boy from a poor family, he didn't have resources that were easily available.

To make a new life, with the courage of a lion, he boarded, *Ererero,* an oil tanker owned by a family of shipping magnates, the Mavroleons. The ship transported my dad across rough seas for 12 months.

To survive, he worked hard as a deck hand, helping the crew as best he could along the journey. As the weeks turned into months, the ship traveled from Greece, to Libya, to Amsterdam, to Venezuela, back to Amsterdam, back to Venezuela, through the Panama Canal and up the coast of California. On his 14th birthday, my dad disembarked in San Francisco. He didn't speak English, he didn't have money, and he didn't know how he would make his life in America.

As the famous American industrialist, Henry Ford said, there are two types of men in the world. There are those who think they can, and there are those who think they can't. "Both men were right," Mr. Ford said. Clearly, my father was a man who thought that he could.

Although only a boy, he had the inner fortitude to grow into a man who would know how to pursue his dreams and overcome pressures, he went on to accomplish great things. Knowing the strength of my grandmother, I credit her for the strength he built upon.

Still, I can't imagine the hardship my father endured—all in pursuit of his dream to build a better life. He made his way to a Greek community in New York, starting on jobs as a dishwasher—doing anything asked of him.

Despite pressures he undoubtedly felt, my dad never stopped seeing all that he could become. With those dreams, he started his career, first as a laborer, then as a business owner. He owned ice cream machines, then restaurants.

He owned a food warehouse business, then he built a construction company. Despite not having a high school education, he supported this country by building businesses that generated millions of dollars in revenues, paid taxes, and supported our family.

Similarly, my mom, Angela, had that same strength. They were one and the same, and for that reason, they could build strength through hardship. Instead of succumbing to the pressures, they always pursued their dreams.

As I've said before, my mother comes from Kos, an island that is famous as the home of Hippocrates, the world's father of modern medicine. When we hear doctors say that the *first rule of medicine is to do no harm*, that is the wisdom of Hippocrates.

Like my father's family, my mother's family was poor—but with 11 children, the large family had to work together.

They lived on a small farm, working hard by raising potatoes, tomatoes, and other vegetables. After the atrocities of war, they wanted to build a better life and made the decision to immigrate to America when my mother was still a child. To get ready they had to follow a plan:

» First my parents would come to settle.

» They would work and learn a bit more about the country.

» They would save money to bring the rest of the family over.

My mother and her siblings had to remain in Greece for a year while my grandparents settled. They lived with extended family, borrowing clothes that did not fit. Once my grandparents saved sufficient funds to buy the plane tickets for my mom and all of her sisters and brothers, the 11 children boarded a plane that flew to America.

My grandfather worked as a dishwasher at a restaurant in New Jersey, earning $180 a week. To supplement the family earnings, my grandmother worked in a textile factory at low wages. Despite the pressures, they made it work, struggling.

Without being able to speak a word of English, my mom started school. She had to brave through the ridicule and prejudice because she didn't speak English. Other kids teased her relentlessly for wearing unfashionable clothes, ridiculing her for wearing "highwaters." Through all of the tears that came with struggle, she grew stronger.

When she was only 15, she met my father. Smitten with her beauty, my dad started to pursue her. In the

Greek tradition, my father went to my mother's home with his father.

They wanted to ease the concern of my mother's parents, assuring them of my dad's honorable intentions. He asked my maternal grandparents for permission to marry my mom. He was 18 and she wasn't yet 16. They started their lives together and began building a family, fueled by dreams, undaunted by the pressures.

Being ambitious, my dad got started with a Mr. Softie ice cream truck. With my mom working by his side, they started to build.

Together they started coffee shops, restaurants, and diners. With my mom's help, by the time my dad was 22 years old, they owned a large restaurant with an amazing bakery. Despite being only 20, and not having a high school education, my mom did everything necessary to keep the restaurant going, including working as the bookkeeper.

Community leaders became so impressed with their restaurant that

The Trentonian newspaper wrote a full profile, highlighting my parents as a model of success—two young immigrants working hard to reach their dreams in America.

Together, my parents built and sold several businesses, while simultaneously raising my three older sisters, Angeliki, Oreanthe, Roula, my brother, Theo, and me.

As the youngest person in the family, I always felt a duty to live up to the leadership I saw in my grandparents, my parents, my older brother and sisters. Love for family, community, and the Greek culture is what continues to fuel my ambition today, and what carried me through the challenges I found along the way.

Plato's Allegory of the Cave:

For all of us, if we want to overcome pressures and achieve our dreams, we must develop the strength of mind to keep pushing forward, even in the face of difficulty. Sometimes, we have to reject what others tell us about what our future could hold. Instead, we have to see what is possible, as we learn from Plato's story on the Allegory of the Cave, in his famous book, The Republic.

Plato's story challenges each of us to learn how to think for ourselves. The story begins by asking us to imagine a group of prisoners. All of the prisoners have lived the entirety of their lives chained to a post in a dark cave. Their legs and their necks were bound to the post in ways that prevented them from turning their heads. As such, they could only see the wall directly in front of them.

Behind the prisoners, there was a natural light source. Between the light source and the prisoners, people sometimes walked, carrying various objects. Shadows from the movement projected along the wall in front of the prisoners.

For their entire lives, those prisoners only saw the shadows moving across the wall in front of them. Since they didn't know anything different, the prisoners thought the shadows moving along the wall in front of them were real objects.

Plato invited his readers to imagine that one of the prisoners escaped from the cave. Somehow, he broke free.

Once free, the former prisoner could walk outside of the cave and see the sunshine. It took a while for his eyes to adjust.

But as he walked around, he began to discover and learn more, to develop a different perspective. He realized that what he had taken to be reality for his entire life were only shadows, projected from a light source that he didn't know had been shining behind him. That knowledge gave him an entirely new perspective on life.

Feeling sorry for his companions that remained back in the cave, the prisoner returned, wanting to enlighten them.

With enthusiasm, he told them what he had discovered. Yet rather than welcoming the enlightened wisdom of their former companion, they rejected him, saying that he had lost his mind. Since he no longer saw the world as they had been conditioned to know the world, they refused to listen to anything he said.

Application to our Life:

Although Plato lived more than 2,000 years ago, we can still take so many lessons from that wisdom and apply that wisdom to our life.

Are we living in the light, or in the cave?

Plato's allegory suggests that people trapped in the cave represent the thinking patterns for the majority of people in the world. They allow others to tell them who they are, how to think, what limitations they have, and what pathway they must take if they want anything different.

Plato's story teaches us that we must learn to think for ourselves, and to work toward overcoming barriers that can block us from success. If we remain stuck in the cave, we miss opportunities and get stuck in mediocrity. Instead of pursuing our own dreams, we live as if we're prisoners, limited by what others say we can become.

Even though more than 2,000 years have passed since Plato wrote *The Republic,* his lessons are as valuable today as they were back then. People have a tendency to live in accordance with how others tell them to live. It's a lazy way of living. Instead, we should be like the prisoner who escaped. We should work to develop our own perspective on the world, figuring out our own pathway to overcome pressures and achieve our dreams.

In Plato's story, the escaped prisoner represents the relatively smaller percentage of people who dare to think and act differently from those in the crowd. Instead of being trapped in a world of "shadows," they venture outside their comfort zones; with courage, they step into the light of their dreams, uncovering the true reality of life—as they create it.

These people—like my parents—are not afraid to cross oceans. No matter how rough the journey, they pursue their dreams. The immediate pressures of life do not deter them, because they always see themselves as being able to achieve something more—to conquer something more.

If a person finds himself in struggle, or in a challenging situation, the answer is not complaining or giving up hope. Rather, the answer lies within, by visualizing what we can become, given the right level of commitment. As stated earlier, we must start by visualizing the best possible outcome. We must set clear goals and make a commitment. But we always must visualize our dreams, knowing that if we apply ourselves, we can become something more.

Getting Back on Track:

When I returned to New York after the disastrous detour to Miami, I had to recalibrate and get back on track—much as I'm doing right now. At any time, life can take us on a turn. We need a strategy to make things right again.

Instead of living like the prisoners of Plato's cave, listening to what others tell us, or believing that we're destined to live with challenge, we must open our mind to what is possible. We must define success independently and create our pathway to succeed. With commitment, we must chart our destiny, pursuing it with a clear vision of our dreams. That strategy can help us overcome the pressure.

In America, we see a lot of people being influenced by trends. Instead of thinking on their own, they follow along as if they're sheep. They do not consider their dreams. They do not consider their strengths and weaknesses.

For example, millions of unmotivated students follow along as if they're "prisoners of a cave," taking on thousands of dollars in student-loan debt to attend college. Instead of applying themselves in college, they goof off, as I did in Miami. They lose their way and put themselves further behind.

College can be a great experience for those who embrace the journey with commitment, and for those who see it as a pathway to a better life. Yet we see many people who go through college for the wrong reasons. Rather than wanting an education to achieve their highest potential, or to pursue success as they define success, they are living someone else's dream, or living in ways that others tell them to live.

My parents taught me that college isn't the only way to build a successful life. From both my mother and father, I saw that a person could come to America without speaking English.

Despite not having an advanced education, a person can choose to develop a good work ethic and discipline. The virtues of a solid work ethic and discipline, together with a strong mindset, could lead people to build lives of meaning, relevance, and dignity. I wanted to emulate success as I saw in the leaders around me. Their secret, as I saw it:

» Rather than focusing on the pressures around them, a person had to clarify the dream, and pursue it gradually, making decisions that aligned with what the person wanted to become—and not what others said they had to do.

My misguided trip to South Florida cost me dearly. I had lost all that I had saved from my years of working through high school and my credit had fallen into arrears. Lenders repossessed the car I'd been driving. With more than $20,000 in credit delinquencies, I couldn't even get a cell phone.

I didn't have any foreseeable way of repaying my debts, and conventional wisdom suggested that I should file bankruptcy and start over.

Yet the leaders that inspired me did not live by conventional wisdom. Instead, they taught me to pursue dreams with commitment. They taught me to think about how I could get my ship back on course, pursuing success with my dignity intact. Bad decisions got me into the problem. Good decisions and commitment would help me make it through.

Healing:

To recalibrate, I went back to my strengths. While in high school, I gained experience by working in neighborhood pharmacies. At Argos Drugs, I learned a lot about customer service.

I got a great sense of fulfillment out of helping people get the medicines they needed to feel better. Although I didn't have the aptitude or desire to return to school and get a medical education, I felt a calling, as inspired by my roots on my mother's island of Kos and the Hippocratic oath.

Wanting to work with people, and to help them feel better, I put a plan together that, I hoped, would lead to a career in the pharmacy business.

From my perspective, I needed career growth, and I looked for an opportunity where I might be able to apply all that I learned previously—and then learn more. I didn't envision myself being in debt and working as a store clerk forever. Wanting something more, I envisioned "the best possible outcome."

My earlier experience with Argos Drugs taught me what I needed to know about serving customers in a small, neighborhood pharmacy. To develop more breadth and depth of knowledge, I needed to work my way into a bigger opportunity. In time, I could see myself as the owner of my own business. That dream gave me the energy I needed to power through the pressures I felt of being in debt.

Lessons for All:

As I'm writing this document, we're in the midst of a changing world. A global pandemic has forced millions of people to rethink what they're doing, and where they're going.

Millions of people have lost their lives. Entire industries have been shut down. Governing authorities have ordered people to stay at home. With those new orders, people have lost paychecks and they've fallen into debt. Each of us has to make a decision on best-possible outcomes.

What is it that we want?

The previous chapters of this book show how I've had to ask that question at various stages of my life. When I was a young boy, a desire to become independent led to my first job at McDonalds. In pursuit of higher earnings, I took a job with Argos Drugs. By saving and living beneath my means,

I succeeded in buying my first car and taking a cross-country trip.

When I defined success clearly, I made progress. By moving to South Florida, I lost sight of that clear vision. Instead of pursuing a specific goal, I got diverted by chasing what others told me I should be doing—having a good time, enjoying my youth with a party scene. That diversion took me off track, put me into a financial bind. To get out, I needed to restore that clarity of thought.

All people face challenges and struggles from time to time. If we don't recalibrate, those challenges and struggles can decimate our spirit and confidence. At any time, we can choose something different. We can pursue our dreams—regardless of what other people tell us is possible.

When authorities brought criminal charges against me, in the fall of 2020, I had to recalibrate again. Like everyone else, I was coping with the pandemic and with other struggles that I'll explain in the chapters ahead.

But a criminal charge represented a problem of an entirely different magnitude. The charge threatened to put my liberty at risk, and for a brief time, I felt overwhelmed with pressure.

» In what ways would those pressures influence my life?

» If I don't do something about my predicament, where will I be in the years to come?

Those questions led me to the solution. Whining about the pressures I faced would not get me through the challenge. Like the Stoics advised, I had to live in the world as it existed— and not as I wanted it to be.

Reflecting on strategies that I learned from leaders gave me the strength to endure. Whether the stories of Homer, the wisdom of Socrates, the philosophy of Plato, or the personal histories of my parents, I knew that I had the power within to make life better. The key would be in doing what I learned from others.

All of us as human beings face challenges, and today. We must make a choice of how we're going to respond. Since I would never ask anyone to do anything that I am not doing, I started to document the pathway, which is what led to this book of my journey. It's my hope that others can use it chart out their own pathway to success when they face challenges in their life:

» Step 1: Define Success

» Step 2: Create the goals to take you from where you are to what you want to become.

» Step 3: Make your commitment

» Step 4: If you need fall off track, recalibrate with a vision of a better outcome

» Step 5: Take incremental action steps

In the next chapter, I'll reveal more on the importance of taking those incremental steps, showing how they worked for me. Incremental steps led me out of debt and positioned me for new opportunities. And incremental steps will help me emerge triumphantly from this criminal charge.

» What incremental steps can you take that will lead you from where you are, to what you aspire to become?

» If challenged by that question, consider the examples I offered in this chapter, including:

» A 13-year old boy who crossed the ocean to pursue dreams in America.

» An eight-year old girl who started school without speaking English, married and started to raise a family before she turned 16.

» A prisoner who escaped from the darkness of a cave to build a new, more fulfilling life.

» And, as you'll see, a young man who emerges from being $20,000 in debt, to becoming a small business owner, employer, and sponsor for building stronger, more vibrant communities.

Incremental Action Steps
Chapter 5

If you intend to reach a higher station in life, then you've got to be willing to climb. To build a pathway to prosperity, learn the importance of taking incremental action steps.

The incremental steps you take today may require discipline and effort, but they will open opportunities that otherwise would not be available to you. This is the way of the world.

Each of us survives in the world because we went through incremental stages of growth. Think about it. By the time we're conceived, we've already overcome enormous challenges.

We go through nine months of development, then when our mothers deliver, we're crying, helpless infants. We're completely dependent on our mothers. In incremental stages, we learn. We learn to get attention, we learn to crawl, we learn to walk, we learn to think, we learn that if we pursue growth in incremental action steps, we can overcome challenges.

When I returned to New York in 2010, I was only 22, but I had a lifetime of maturity behind me. I learned lessons by listening, observing, and experiencing.

For this reason, I've never regretted the losses I suffered by taking that detour to Miami. Traveling without a plan led to the loss of savings I'd accumulated through earlier work and the lack of a plan sank me into debt.

Yet it also taught a valuable lesson that I cherish to this day. It wasn't the best decision for financial reasons, or for career decisions. Yet the experience helped to shape me, or mold me into becoming the man that I am today.

By losing everything, I got a valuable lesson—to never give up, to never stop living in accordance with values and goals. But if I do lose my way,

I learned that I could always get back on track. Anyone can do the same!

If you're going through a challenging time, consider the lessons that you can learn from the experience.

Then, start taking the incremental steps that will help you grow into the person you aspire to become. Take steps that will take you from where you are today to the success you want to achieve in the months, years, and decades to come.

As we learned from Plato's Allegory of the Cave, we don't have to take the traditional route, nor do we have to live in accordance with what everyone else expects of us.

If we know what we want to achieve, we can engineer our own pathway to succeed. The incremental action steps we take today will open opportunities that we may not even be able to contemplate.

Through this chapter, I'll show how I considered strengths and weaknesses when making the plan that helped me climb from struggle to prosperity, in incremental steps. Again, when I returned to New York, I had two big weaknesses: I didn't have any money, and I owed creditors $20,000.

But I also had strengths, including a good work ethic, a commitment to overcome, and knowledge about retail pharmacy sales. From the lessons I learned, I understood that I would have to take a series of incremental action steps to climb back to stability.

Early Steps:

The right job may not be the right decision for everyone. For me, getting the right job would be an essential first decision. Let me put an emphasis on making it "*the right job*." Why? Because choosing a career path is an essential choice for anyone.

When we choose a job, we make a life choice. Every decision comes with opportunity costs. Once we take a job, we miss out on opportunities for other jobs. We can get stuck in some type of activity that cuts us off from other options.

While pursuing excitement in Miami, for example, I got cut off from the advancement that I otherwise could have been making. Similarly, when others go into massive debt to enroll in university programs that won't have any relationship to what they become in life, they miss out on opportunities that may otherwise help them succeed.

With this end in mind, I gave a lot of thought to how I wanted to resume my life once I settled in at my parents' house.

Take note of that. Rather than going into further debt by renting a place I could not afford, when I returned from Florida, I moved back in with my parents. That incremental step represented a commitment to get my financial house back in order. I'd have to take steps on two fronts:

1. I would have to live frugally,

2. I would have to create an employment opportunity.

The opportunity would allow me to earn a sufficient income to repay my debt. The job would have to build upon my previous experience, while simultaneously putting me on a pathway that would lead to fulfillment in life.

I needed a plan.

I'm inspired by wisdom we attribute to President Abraham Lincoln. Essentially, President Lincoln advised that if given six hours to chop down a tree, the best approach would be to spend the first five hours planning and sharpening the axe.

We've all got to plan and sharpen our axe when striving to resolve our problems. Before going out to look for a job, I "planned and sharpened my axe" by researching the best potential places to work. It would not make sense to simply go after the first job—I had to find *the right job.*

Although I felt confident that many local, neighborhood pharmacies near our home in Flushing would hire me, a small, local pharmacy wouldn't be the best fit, given the stage I was in.

At 22 years old, I wanted to pursue a specific pathway that would allow me to feel good about my work, but also help me overcome some of the challenges in my life.

Small neighborhood pharmacies would neither offer the type of growth potential I needed, nor would they allow me to learn more. I had to expand my depth and breadth of knowledge.

Since I derived a great deal of satisfaction by helping people, another option would have been to work for one of the big-chain pharmacies, like a CVS or a Right Aid. But I couldn't take that path. In fact, I detested the large, retail pharmacies.

From what I could see, the large pharmacies were way too impersonal, and they charged customers way too much without providing the kind of personalized service that people deserved.

As a Greek, I place enormous value on human relationships and community. As Hippocrates taught us, the first rule of healing is to do no harm.

To do no harm, a person must truly devote himself to knowing as much as possible about the people we're serving.

The big-chain pharmacies were like retail stores, carrying thousands of items but not placing any emphasis on providing a personalized experience for the customers they served. People who work in those types of pharmacies don't develop any connection with the neighborhood. Building better communities didn't matter nearly as much as profits to the big-chain stores. I didn't want to devote my life to a pharmacy that didn't put people and community first.

I admired learning the personality of customers and the personality of owners. As a consumer, and as a person that once worked in an independent pharmacy, I noticed a massive difference from the large chain pharmacies. Independent pharmacies lived and breathed with the community.

For example, if the owner was Polish, and served a Polish neighborhood, he would carry products that his customers recognized and wanted. Similarly, if the owner was Spanish, serving a Spanish community, he would carry ethnic products for the people in his community.

When I worked at Argos Drugs, some of the wellness products had the type of Greek labels that I saw in my grandmother's cabinets; Greek people went to Argos because they felt a connection to the owner and to the store. The chain pharmacies, in contrast, only carried big brands, like Johnson and Johnson.

I liked independent pharmacies because the owners invested heavily to build a stronger connection with the people. With that stronger connection, we could get more personal and help more people.

Like Abraham Lincoln advised, I highly recommend people should *prepare and sharpen their axe* before they set out to solve a problem.

If a person is thinking about developing a career, start by researching, or planning. Consider the type of job or business that will bring the most happiness and fulfillment. Planning and researching is an essential first step on the long path toward becoming successful.

In creating my plan and preparing, I had to think about what I knew. For example:

» I didn't have a car, so I wouldn't be able to drive,

» I didn't want to work in a small pharmacy near our home in Flushing,

» I didn't want to work in a large chain-store type pharmacy,

» I wanted to develop skills that I didn't have,

» I wanted to work in a place that would help me solve my financial problems, but also one that might open more opportunities might open later.

By thinking first about my strengths, my weaknesses, and what I wanted to accomplish, I could create a more methodical plan. Anyone who wanted to resolve a problem or achieve a more intentional outcome could use this same strategy that I used to make my plan.

Knowing what I wanted, I began researching on the Internet, looking at the subway system in New York. I had to think about commuting time, since I didn't want my commute to last longer than 40 minutes, I drew a big circle to identify the right areas where I should search.

I contemplated areas that would open the best opportunities—given the type of pharmacy where I wanted to work. Once I found the location, I went to the "Maps" section on Google. By typing *pharmacy* and the zip code for the area that interested me, a list of stores began popping up. I went down the list starting to make my calls to pharmacies in Manhattan.

When I made the call, I asked to speak with the pharmacist. Why? Because I knew that in most cases, the person answering the phone wouldn't really have any decision-making power.

If I called to say I was looking for a job, I would likely get the runaround. The person would likely tell me that the manager was busy. On the other hand, by asking to speak with the pharmacist, the person answering the phone would consider me a customer.

Without hesitation, the person answering the phone would transfer me to the owner of the pharmacy, or someone with authority.

When the pharmacist picked up, I'd introduced myself politely and inquired whether the store had any interest in hiring an experienced, disciplined, and dependable employee.

That proved to be a good conversation starter. The first person I called told me that he was nearing retirement and about to sell his pharmacy.

But he asked whether I understood the computer system that pharmacist's use, and if I knew how to fulfill prescriptions. When I confirmed that I worked in a neighborhood pharmacy for longer than seven years, he gave me the phone number of his son, David, who was opening a new pharmacy in the Dumbo area of Brooklyn.

After getting David's contact information, I looked up the location of City Chemist, at 104 Jay Street. It was within walking distance of the York Street Subway Station.

I'd have about a 30-minute commute from Flushing, which wasn't bad. When I spoke with David, he asked me a few questions. I responded to his satisfaction, assuring him that I would be available from the time the store opened until the time the store closed, and I would work without days off.

A pharmacist wants efficiency. When he is fulfilling prescriptions, he is busy. He needs to cultivate a team that will carry out other functions of the store when he is working with people that need medications. That team should be self-directed, using critical-thinking skills to improve efficiencies for the customers.

In building his team, a pharmacist doesn't want to have to train too many people. It's a lot of work to bring a person up to speed with all of the products, and the way of operations. Since I wasn't attending college, and I didn't have children, I confirmed that the pharmacy would be able to count on me as a dedicated and reliable member of the team; I would be willing to work as many hours as possible.

Further, since I wanted to learn, the owners could count on me to help out in every way possible. He liked my responses and invited me to come in for an interview.

When I pitched my strengths—that I was young, filled with energy, and dependable—the partners liked my enthusiasm. After some small talk, they saw that I could be an asset to the pharmacy, and they hired me on the spot. I started working that first day, grateful for the opportunity.

With about 5,000 square feet, City Chemist was really best-in-class when it came to a neighborhood pharmacy. In the front, the store carried really high-end cosmetics, with all of the best brands. In the back, the pharmacist worked to fulfill prescriptions and carried over-the-counter medications. I got to know everything, starting by stocking shelves and keeping the place clean.

Second Step: Providing Real Value

As soon as I started, I took initiative. By taking responsibility to clean shelves and organize products, I got real product knowledge. Further, I could make things operate more efficiently, by putting items in a place that would be most efficient for the customers.

I organized a children's section, a section for cold medicines, a section for wellness products. The owners appreciated my initiative, seeing that I wanted to make things most convenient for the customers.

Since the store was close to the train station, every day a wave of people would come in. I got to know the customers, so that I could be personable but also efficient. During the first two years, I worked double shifts, seven days a week, including holidays.

By working so many hours, never taking a day off, and living frugally, I earned enough money to pay off the $20,000 I owed to creditors within two years—even though my hourly wage was less than $20.

Once I paid off my debt, I started to take one day off a week, Tuesdays, because that day had the least amount of traffic; I wanted to be available to help every other day.

While working at City Chemist, I learned everything possible about running an effective retail store. By interacting with people, we learn how to treat them, we learn that the customer is always right.

My job wasn't only to clean and organize, but to make the people feel comfortable by giving them the most efficient, pleasant experience. I learned how to order and what to order. I learned how to manage inventory.

My job duties included filling prescriptions, calling doctors, putting inventory into the computer system and keeping track of how well different products sold.

Every day before we closed, I'd walk through the store, a computer in hand, taking notes on what we needed to order and straightening out all of the shelves.

This daily commitment made me intimately familiar with every aspect of the store's operations. The more I knew about the business, the more effectively I could provide service to the customers and ease responsibilities for the owners.

With success of the first store in the Dumbo neighborhood, the owners opened a second story, in

Brooklyn Heights, at 120 Montague Street. When they took possession of the store, the owners tasked me with helping to set up.

By starting with a blank slate, I could learn a great deal more, like how to set up the shelving, and how to lay our inventory out in a way that made the most sense for consumers.

When I began my job search, I set a goal of expanding my depth and breadth of knowledge. Working with City Chemist helped me to fulfill that ambition.

I got to know the suppliers of all the resources that were necessary to

---

operate a pharmacy. By working with them well, I could take enormous responsibilities off the owner's plate. In many ways, I felt as if I were a part of the team.

Although I only earned an hourly wage, I derived a great sense of satisfaction in learning. It was as if I were growing through a specialized training program that would position me for new opportunities later.

In an effort to build more community engagement, I set up one area of the store to support local community merchants. If someone from the neighborhood created a product and wanted to sell it in our store, we would accept the product on consignment and donate profits to a charity. These tactics led to great relationships and customer loyalty. People would go out of their way to spend time with us.

For example, Richard Hunt, one of the customers, made an enormous impression on me. An older man, in his mid 80s, he would spend time walking along Montague Street every day, visiting the cafes or breakfast shops.

Since he came into our store several times each week, I befriended him. On weekends, he would bring his breakfast in and eat with me. I cleared off a little area of the shelving and let him relax in our store to read his newspapers. When my schedule wasn't too busy, I'd sit down to listen and learn from him. Those kinds of human relationships are priceless to me, and the reason I wanted to be in the healing business.

Richard told me that he'd never been married, never had children. His family consisted of several brothers and sisters, most of whom had died. He'd lost touch with the others, as more than 10 years had passed since he spoke with anyone in his family.

I felt grateful for an opportunity to bring him a little joy, listening as he told me about the life he lived as a merchant marine, traveling to ports far away, like Thailand, China, Australia, or even Greece.

One day, right before the holidays, he came by the store as he always did. Since Richard hadn't come in for a while, I worried about him. Sounding incoherent and confused, he didn't seem normal. Knowing that he lived alone, without any family to look after him, I called an ambulance to assess him.

After diagnosing him in the pharmacy, the medics took him to a hospital for testing. They concluded that he had water in his lungs. After he got better, he asked if I would serve as his healthcare proxy. I agreed. Rather than discharging him, the hospital wanted to send him to a rehab facility—but he didn't want to go.

Since Richard had been a friend of the pharmacy, and a friend of mine, I took the initiative to help out, finding him a home-health assistant. She would go to his house and help with anything he needed, like grocery shopping and so forth.

Within a week, Richard fell and hurt his head. An ambulance brought him to the hospital, and the doctor told me he was listed as a "Do-Not-Resuscitate." Knowing that he wanted to live, I instructed the doctors that I was his healthcare proxy and they should do what they could to help him live.

Caring for people brought me a real sense of meaning. To care for Richard, I thought about what I could do to make his final days in the hospital more pleasant. I coordinated for a priest to come and read him last rights.

I also brought him a bottle of Dr. Pepper, his favorite soda. While sitting next to him, I fed him the soda by pouring it into a teaspoon and giving him one spoonful at a time. That effort cheered him up and made him grow stronger.

Knowing that he took great pride in his appearance, and that he liked to be clean shaven, I brought shaving cream and a trimmer, which he appreciated.

After two weeks of visiting him in the hospital, I felt really sad that he didn't have anyone else in the world.

Remembering that Richard told me that he had a brother named Charlie, and that they were from the community of Pittsfield, Massachusetts, I took it upon myself to find his brother.

By doing some simple online research, I narrowed down about 20 potential names, then started to dial the phone numbers. "My name is Demetri," I said, "and I'm calling on behalf of Richard Hunt, who has a brother named Charles. Is this the same Charles that has a brother named Richard Hunt who lives in Brooklyn?"

"You mean Dickie," the first person I called asked. I couldn't believe it. I got lucky on the first try. Charles told me that he hadn't seen his brother in longer than 20 years. Once we established the sibling connection, I told Charles about Richard's health and suggested that he may want to come visit him before he passed.

Charles came to visit, and he brought Richard back with him to Massachusetts. They got to spend a couple of weeks together before Richard passed away, and I felt grateful that I could play a role in bringing them happiness. That type of personal service wouldn't exist in a big-chain pharmacy, and it brought more satisfaction than financial rewards.

The owners appreciated my commitment to making City Chemist a true neighborhood resource. But just as much as I gave to the store, the owners gave back to me.

When they opened a third store and a fourth store, I got to help them build. By the time they opened the fifth store, they invited me to make an investment so that I could become an owner. Their invitation showed their appreciation for the high level of commitment I made to growing their amazing business.

The salient point, I think, is that if we pursue a methodical path to overcoming our challenges, we can succeed. Consider the blueprint that I offered, and let's continue building it:

» Step 1: Define Success

» Step 2: Create the goals to take you from where you are to what you want to become.

» Step 3: Make your commitment

» Step 4: If you fall off track, recalibrate with a vision of a better outcome

» Step 5: Take incremental action steps

If I didn't adhere to that methodical plan, and take those incremental steps, I may never have been able to overcome the setback I had by moving to Florida.

I may never have been able to repay the $20,000 that I owed to creditors. I may never have been able to learn everything there was to know about opening and operating a neighborhood pharmacy that served its people in a highly personal way, as I did with Richard Hunt.

Without those incremental steps, the owners of City Chemist never would have invited me to invest to be-come an owner in their firm.

That leads me to the next lesson on the pathway to success, which is measuring progress. I'll cover that step in the next chapter.

I encourage you to think these steps through in your own life. Learn how to chart your path from where you are today, to a higher level of sat-isfaction and fulfillment.

Measuring Progress
Chapter 6

At any time, we can think back to see how yesterday's decisions influenced who and what we've become. If we reflect, we should see that when we acted intentionally, we grew stronger.

When we lost our way, or took steps without clear intention, we sometimes spun out of control. At least that's what I experienced, as previous chapters have shown.

A move to Florida put me on the wrong track that didn't lead me in the direction I wanted. Fortunately, I used a disciplined strategy that included measuring progress.

By measuring progress, I could reverse course and get back on track. Others should see that if they're not happy with where their life is right now, they can use this same strategy to recalibrate and choose a different direction—just like leaders have done throughout history.

To lessen the chance of falling off track—or making decisions that could deter us from achieving our goals— we should create a personal strategy.

By continuously assessing where we are at a given stage and contrasting that assessment with where we want to be at various points in our future, we can stay on track. This personal-growth strategy of measuring progress can help us grow into the type of people we aspire to become.

Accountability metrics become useful tools in all areas of life. The more we understand how to use them, the more we can depend upon them to get back on track when things aren't going quite the way we want.

For example, in an earlier chapter, I wrote about my experiences in high school. When I started high school, my parents told me an education would open new opportunities. But I didn't really embrace the message.

Sitting in a classroom just didn't feel right for me and I didn't like that style of "book" learning. Some people do really well in school. But growing up as the youngest son in an entrepreneurial Greek family, I had to learn how to speak up and go after what I wanted.

I preferred to learn by actively participating in anything I was doing. It didn't matter if I was on vacation in Greece, learning about the importance of conservation, community service, and humility from my grandmother, or working at McDonald's cleaning bathrooms. I found lessons in all work that would help me grow.

I learned about customer service and developing a good work ethic by being friendly to people and measuring progress on the jobs that I did.

As a result of not doing well in school, teachers told me that I kept falling further behind in school. They used their own accountability metrics to track my progress.

When my report cards didn't measure up, the administrators transferred me from a regular school to a night school. Once I started attending the classes in night school, I immediately saw how I'd fallen onto the wrong track.

Although I knew that I was never going to be a gifted student in a formal academic program, I could see that I would have to make some changes. I felt determined to cross the minimum threshold of earning a high school degree, but I didn't want to attend school in a threatening environment.

To change course, I started to apply myself. I continued working on my job at Argos Drugs, but I wasn't going to abandon my commitment to earning a high school diploma.

Believing that a high school diploma would become a resource I could use throughout my life, I took the measurable steps necessary to get back to a school with regular day-time classes. Every day, I kept track of the assignments I needed to complete in order to catch up with expectations from my teachers. That strategy helped me along with the incremental steps I had to take in order to succeed.

Experience has taught me lessons on the importance of measuring progress, and these lessons helped me any time that decisions took me off track. Life doesn't always move along in a straight line to success.

Although we strive to make progress, we sometimes make decisions that lead to setbacks—as I experienced with my trip to Florida. A real-time example of a set back I encouraged with my arrest, and the challenges I'm facing with the criminal justice system. These setbacks came as a result of my own decisions.

Other times, we go through setbacks that come through no fault of our own. For example, millions of people work in restaurants, bars, clubs, movie theaters, or other businesses that have been shuttered because of the global pandemic. The point is that we all suffer setbacks, and we can choose to create our own tools to get back on track.

If we create mechanisms for measuring progress, we strengthen ourselves in two ways. First, we build tools to help us assess where we are and where we want to go, within specified timelines.

Second, this tool becomes an insurance policy for us, helping us to stay on course or to know when we have to change course. We know that if we keep moving in the right direction, we're going to overcome our challenges. It may take time and effort, but we'll overcome our challenges if we adhere to this strategy.

Throughout the journey of our life, we're going to make mistakes and suffer setbacks. Any time we see that we're not in the position we'd like—as I'm experiencing right now with my arrest—we can set new goals. As the Stoic philosophers advised us, we choose how we live.

We can choose to live in the world as it exists and be happy, or we can choose to be miserable because of problems we encounter in life. Those problems may come from our own making, or from circumstances that are beyond our ability to control.

We can always choose how to respond. Experience has taught me that when life changes for the worse, we should redefine success, given the changed circumstances. Then we should take incremental steps to set new goals we want to achieve. If we measure progress along the way, we empower ourselves and grow stronger every day.

Success comes when we understand that there are certain problems we have to solve along the way. If I had not solved my problems when I returned from Florida, I would have remained in a cycle of struggle. But by laying out a plan, I could overcome challenges in incremental stages. I had to measure progress along the way. The little steps I took led to bigger opportunities that otherwise would never have opened for me.

This strategy of measuring progress motivated me to work harder while I climbed through the challenges I faced when I moved back to New York. After finding the right job and persuading the owners at City Chemist to hire me, I held myself accountable to work as many hours as possible.

I wanted to stay on track so that I could pay off my debt, restore my credit, and learn as much as possible about operating a successful retail business. But I had bigger plans as well. To get there, I had to go step by step, making progress within a clear timeline that I set.

Once the owners of City Chemist hired me, I knew exactly what I needed to do. By measuring my incremental progress, I could keep a high level of energy every day. I had a routine, waking up at 6:50 every morning. By 7:30, I was out the door so that I could catch the train and open the pharmacy on time.

I'd work all day and close the store at 8:00 in the evening, then ride the train home. By 9:00, I'd get home, exhausted but grateful for leading a full and productive day. I'd spend time with my family, get some rest, and wake with both happiness and gratitude because I kept measuring the progress.

I understood that if I stayed on the path, I would put my credit problems behind me and start working toward higher levels of success.

By paying down my debts, a few hundred dollars with each paycheck, I saw my credit starting to improve. That credit report became one of my accountability tools. I could see the scores improve, and I knew how crucial those credit scores would be to my future. When I first returned from New York, my credit scores were so low that I couldn't even qualify to sign up for a cellphone plan. With regular payments, I resolved that problem.

Once I paid off all of my debts, I started to rely upon an even more inspiring way to measure progress—the balances in my growing savings account.

Those balances started to grow in hundred-dollar increments at first. I smiled when I saw the balance exceed $1,000 for the first time. Several months later, with disciplined deposits, the balance grew to exceed $10,000. More time passed, and more deposits. The balance grew to exceed $50,000. Then, a few years later, I watched my bank balance grow to surpass $100,000.

Despite wages that never exceeded $25 per hour, the job at City Chemist opened an opportunity for me to change my life. I simply had to stay on the path of slow-and-steady, incremental growth. I had to measure the progress every day. An accountability log gave me the discipline to avoid get-rich-quick schemes.

Instead of chasing investments that I couldn't fully control, I kept working more hours, and putting every paycheck I made toward the goals that I set. By measuring the slow-and-steady progress along the way, I had the discipline to keep going.

Although I could spend the money I was earning or saving, by measuring the progress toward goals I set, I got a huge source of satisfaction that kept my energy level high.

Some people complain about working 40-hour work weeks, even though in reality, those 40-hour work weeks don't amount to much more than 30-hours of work.

To build a better life, we've got to change the way we look at what we're doing. By defining success, setting clear goals, making a commitment, we can achieve so much more than if we simply punch a timecard. By measuring our progress regularly, I've learned that we can achieve a higher potential.

During the seven years that City Chemist employed me, I averaged more than 70 hours of work each week. From my perspective, every hour that I worked felt like an investment in the future I wanted to build. That commitment grew my savings to exceed $200,000, all from hourly wages that I earned on the job.

Those steady accomplishments boosted my confidence, and I always shared the progress I made with the owners of City Chemist.

They encouraged me. In many ways, their leadership inspired me to work harder. When they hired me, I spoke honestly with them, telling them how some bad decisions led me into debt. From the start, I pledged to devote myself with relentless work so that I could get back on track.

A lot of people talk about wanting to transform their life, but they never do more than give the "happy talk." The owners at City Chemist paid me the highest compliment when they invited me to invest alongside them, so that I could become a part owner of the fifth store they were going to open.

Making Best Decisions:

I put a great deal of thought into the possibility of buying an ownership stake with City Chemist. To be clear, the owners were not offering to let me buy a part of the whole company.

My contribution would only grant me a 10% equity stake in the new store. Although it would be a great steppingstone, there would be some drawbacks that I had to consider. The investment would deplete a pot of savings that I had worked hard to build over many years.

What would be the best decision?

To answer that question, I stuck with the strategy I'd been using ever since I returned from Miami. After defining success, I started to lay out my accountability metrics—weighing which option would yield the better return.

I could invest to purchase a 10% equity stake in a new store. Yet I had another option, which would be to use the savings I had accumulated to open my own store and own a 100% equity stake.

There was a great deal to consider. As an established pharmacy, with four operating stores, City Chemist had a solid customer base. In each of those stores, the owners followed a model, with a high-end beauty section in the front, and a full-service pharmacy in the back.

Since I'd been working closely with the owners, I had a good idea of the sales that came from both the beauty side of the store, and the pharmacy. Although I didn't have all the details, such as the costs to operate the business, or the profit margins, I had a good sense of the store's viability.

On the plus side, if I invested with City Chemist, the store would have higher prospects for success. Customers knew the store, and the owners had relationships with many vendors that would also supply the new store. Although no one could guarantee how a new store would perform, with a recipe that had proven to work well in four existing stores, the chances for success would be good.

But how would I define success?

I had a deep admiration and respect for the four owners of City Chemist. Clearly, they were good businessmen who had done well for themselves. By buying into the partnership of a single store, I understood my limitations.

I did not delude myself into believing that the owners would consider me their equal. With only a 10-percent ownership stake of a single store, in a chain of five stores, I wouldn't have the power to make important decisions. The other owners may have respected me as an honest and devoted employee, but I didn't expect them to consider me as an equal partner. In many ways, I would likely be a glorified employee, without much in the way of managerial power.

Accepting the position, to me, would be like opening Pandora's box. According to the Greek poet Hesiod, the king of the gods, Zeus, gave Pandora a box with instructions to care for it—but he forbade Pandora from opening the box, or even looking inside.

Pandora lacked the strength to fight off the temptation. Upon opening the box, all types of problems followed. Despite Pandora's efforts to undo what she had done, there was no way to undo the damage.

The owner's may have had the best of intentions when they offered an opportunity for me to buy a small equity stake into a single store. But the more I thought about the value proposition, the more I thought it would become the equivalent of my "Pandora's Box." It could bring a lot of problems in the way I felt about myself.

After all, I would have invested nearly all of the savings I had accumulated, but I didn't think that I would have a real sense of ownership. I had to think about where I was at the time, and where I wanted to be in five years, or ten years. I needed to hold myself accountable for the level of success I wanted to build.

Clearly, the savings I accumulated, and the knowledge I acquired over the many years that I devoted to City Chemist, put me in a different position from when I started.

When I took the job, heavy debts hung over my head, which limited my options. I could either hang my head low and complain about difficulties from the problems I created, or I could do something to change my situation. I chose to do something—just as I encourage every unhappy person to work in measurable ways to bring positive changes to his or her life.

Getting started toward change after a difficult time is not easy. It's like trying to spin a heavy merry-go-round. Pushing the merry-go-round in one direction will take a lot of energy at the start.

But once the merry-go-round starts spinning, it builds momentum of its own. Turning it round and round requires less energy. That's the way I felt once I started making progress.

Paying down my debts felt hard at first. After I started to watch the balances of debt that I owed begin to drop, I could see the progress. We've all got to work toward what we want to become, and by measuring our progress, we can sustain the energy we need.

Once I decided against investing with the team at City Chemist, I started to consider other options. I didn't want to have any partners. My parents built many businesses by using their own hard work and ingenuity.

Although it may have been easier for them if they would have had partners, they always took the path of being a partner to each other, and to our family.

Through discipline and a good work ethic, they could build businesses on their own. I could take what I learned from them, and also what I learned from my experience at City

Chemist to build a business that would work for me.

To build a business, I simply needed to follow the path. I needed to define success, I needed to lay out my plan, I needed to make a commitment, and I needed to create tools that I could use to hold myself accountable.

For years I'd been learning how to operate a pharmacy. And from City Chemist, I learned that it would be possible to own a pharmacy—even though a person didn't have a pharmacy degree.

This goes back to that lesson I wrote about in the previous chapter, the lesson from Plato's Allegory of the Cave.

We may be conditioned by what others tell us to believe, and not by what is reality. Up until I began working at City Chemist, I thought that a person would need to be a pharmacist to own a pharmacy.

At Argos Drugs, the owner was a pharmacist. He came from a long line of well-educated, medical professionals. Similarly, when I first reached out to City Chemist, I spoke with Alan, who is a pharmacist.

Later, I spoke with his son David, who also was a pharmacist. Later, I learned the other owners of City Chemist did not have pharmacy degrees. As it turned out, a person could own a pharmacy as long as the person employed a pharmacist who would be the pharmacist of record for the store.

This knowledge brought me "out of the cave" and into the light! It gave me insight into new possibilities. Perhaps I could take what I had learned over the many years that I worked at City Chemist, and then take new steps to open my own pharmacy. This option would not have been available if I hadn't prepared myself well, measuring progress every step of the way.

When I decided against investing with the owners of City Chemist, I simultaneously made the decision to go out on my own. I felt ready, as I'd learned a great deal from those leaders and from my experience—for example, I learned how to work well with both customers and with employees.

During the time I worked at City Chemist, I estimate that more than 70 people started and then quit. When I ran my own store, I didn't want to have that high volume of employee turnover. For one thing, customers didn't like to see new people every time they came into the store. We were there to serve them, and we needed to provide a holistic service.

Providing a holistic service meant bringing the people a level of comfort. They were trusting us with knowledge of their health and medical needs. If I were a customer who counted on working with one person, and I trusted him with my medical condition, I wouldn't want to have to go into the pharmacy the next time and have to bring another person up to speed on the necessary medications I needed.

If customers continue to see new employee faces in the store, they will not build that high level of trust and loyalty to the store. Customers could go anywhere if they wanted an impersonal experience.

I put a high value on developing those customer relationships and building trust with them. Those relationships I created went a long way toward building stability for the owners of City Chemist. For example, as a dedicated employee, I got to know many influential people, including Bruce Ratner, the famous real estate developer and community leader who was an owner of the Brooklyn Nets basketball team.

By cultivating that relationship with him, Mr. Ratner helped us secure an opportunity for the beauticians we employed at City Chemist to become makeup artists for the cheerleaders when the Nets played at home. Similarly, I got to know local residents, like Hamish Maxwell, who had been CEO of Philip Morris.

In spending time with customers, I could listen and learn. Whether customers were like Richard Hunt, who was a down-to-earth blue-collar worker, or powerful people like Hamish Maxwell and Bruce Ratner, I could see the value in every human being.

I could treat them with respect and dignity at all times, learn what they needed and strive to serve them. I could open opportunities to show everyone on our team how we respected them. By supporting local businesses and community interest groups, I believed that I could build trust.

All of these lessons began for me when I was a child, whether with my parents or with my grandmother in Greece. They continued when I began working and while I attended school.

When I made a mistake or a bad decision, I could recalibrate and get back on track. If I measured progress in incremental stages, I could go forward. In time, I could solve little problems. By solving those problems,

I could put myself on a path to a better life. I simply had to measure progress every step of the way.

Now that I'm going through these new challenges, I'm documenting the strategies in ways that will help others reach their highest potential. It's part of the way that I'm recalibrating. To build trust, I know that I can never ask anyone to do anything that I'm not doing.

As this story continues, readers will see how I'm using this same strategy today—and how they can use the same blueprint in their life.

» Step 1: Define Success,

» Step 2: Create the goals to take you from where you are to what you want to become,

» Step 3: Make your commitment,

» Step 4: If you fall off track, recalibrate with a vision of a better outcome,

» Step 5: Take incremental action steps, and

» Step 6: Measure Progress.

In the next chapter, we'll go over the next step—which requires us to keep our head in the game!

Keeping our Head in the Game
Chapter 7

What can we learn from Daedalus and Icarus.?

I may not have attended college, but I've learned a great deal about humility from Greek mythology. King Minos had resources to bring the best architects to design and build any structure he wanted. He chose Daedalus, the most skillful craftsman, to build his palace. Besides the palace, the king wanted an elaborate, underground prison.

He instructed Daedalus and his son Icarus to build the labyrinth so King Minos could banish his nemesis, the Minotaur, an evil killing creature that was half-man, half-bull.

After they built the labyrinth, King Minos rewarded both Daedalus and his son Icarus by locking them in the underground maze. That way, King Minos reasoned, it would be impossible for anyone locked inside to ever know how to get out.

Being ingenious, Daedalus came up with an idea on how to escape. He and Icarus gathered feathers from birds and glued them together with wax, making four large wings.

They tied the wings to each shoulder and miraculously, they were able to fly from the labyrinth. They intended to fly over the ocean and escape to the island of Crete, beyond the reach of King Minos.

Before flying, Daedalus warned Icarus not to fly too close to the sun. If he got too close to the sun, Daedalus warned, the wax would melt. Despite the warning, Icarus loved flying and he began to play, going higher and higher. Forgetting his father's lessons, Icarus soared to toward the sun.

As anticipated, the sun melted the wax that held the wings together. When the wings broke apart, Icarus fell into the sea and drowned.

» Moral: When pursuing success, don't get too full of yourself, and don't fly too high!

Since it was one of my favorite Greek myths, I kept Icarus in mind when I made my decision to launch my own pharmacy.

Not knowing precisely how to start, I considered all of my strengths, all of my weaknesses, all of my opportunities, and all of my threats. Anyone could use this same strategy to make better decisions.

» Strengths:

With more than $200,000 in the bank, I felt much stronger than when I began working with City Chemist. Although I was only 29, and didn't have a university degree, I had experience of more than ten years working with consumers.

I understood how to treat people, how to give personal service. The experience helped me to grasp more about what people wanted from a local, independent pharmacy. I wanted to serve those people, and I intended to do so.

» Weakness:

Although I had a solid savings account in the bank, I knew the resources had taken a lifetime for me to accumulate. There is an old saying telling us that we can't have our cake and eat it too.

Once I deployed the savings to open my first pharmacy, I wouldn't have anything remaining. The thought of going through all that money scared me a little bit. I understood the importance of every decision.

If I invested my funds to start a store, and the store didn't succeed, I would be back to ground zero. It's one of the reasons I still cherish the lessons that came from losing everything and going into debt as a result of my move to Florida.

» Opportunities:

People respond to kindness in their community, at every level. Starting an independent, neighborhood pharmacy, I could continue my journey of striving to live as a good citizen—showing appreciation for the blessings that have come our way. These lessons I learned would help me grow.

My grandmother taught me the importance of living as a good member of the community; from my mother and the Hippocratic oath of our island of Kos, I remembered that "We strive to do no harm when helping other people;" and from my father, I understood the power of persistence.

Like Odysseus, I would have to keep going, even during challenging times.

» Threats:

We live in a changing world. Big retailers like CVS, Rite-Aid, and Duane Reade conspire to put the small, independently owned pharmacies out of business.

Now, even the giant Amazon corporation is moving into the pharmaceutical space. From what I was reading, it seemed as if Amazon wanted to decimate the local, independently owned pharmacy industry, just as the giant corporation killed off the local bookstore industry.

It was like the story of David and Goliath! But I felt like David, with a 100% commitment to slaying Goliath with the business I intended to build.

In going into business for myself, I had to consider all of those threats.

When I left City Chemist to launch my first pharmacy, I started with my eyes wide open, keeping my head fully in the game at all times. Despite being a person without any college experience, by following the principles I learned from leaders, I succeeded in building a successful business in the highly regulated industry of dispensing pharmaceutical drugs.

Since I didn't come from a wealthy family, or from a background of university learning, I got my lessons from down-to-earth people, and from the stories that shaped me while growing up, like the Allegory of the Cave, the story of Theseus, of Odysseus, and of Icarus.

We can learn a great deal if we invest the time to think, to plan, and to make deliberate decisions. The key to success, I think, is really about keeping our head in the game—and *Greek Thinking!*

I'm convinced that anyone could achieve higher career goals—as long as they're willing to adhere to the same principled path that leaders taught me, and that I'm sharing with readers of this book.

» My First Store:

Taking my strengths, weaknesses, opportunities, and threats into consideration, I ventured out to find the location for my first store. Before investing money, I had to invest time. It's the same strategy I used when I returned from Miami, when I was deeply in debt and not knowing where I would work.

At the time, I knew I needed the right job. The right job would give me an opportunity to work my way out of debt, to learn more about the pharmacy business, which intrigued me.

We grow stronger when we know what we want. Knowing what we want allows us to take the first action steps that will take us from where we are to where we want to go. We don't need to spend four years in college to get that message.

We simply need to assess whether we like our life as we're living it today. If we don't, we need to think about what we want to become. Then we lay out a map we can follow. With the map, we start taking one step at a time to move closer to success.

And we have to take the right steps at the right time. It wouldn't have made sense for me to go out looking for a store to rent when I first got back from Miami—because I wasn't ready. First, I had to get out of debt and clear up my credit problems. Then I had to build savings and learn more. Once ready, I had to make that commitment and start taking action.

In 2014, feeling ready, I started to make inquiries of how much it would cost to rent space. The owners of City Chemist operated stores of about 5,000-square feet. Those stores were in some of the best neighborhoods, including Dumbo, Brooklyn Heights, Southampton, East Hampton, and other great locations.

When I went to the nicer neighborhoods in Manhattan, and I called landlords, they told me the monthly rent would exceed $30,000! Those inquiries gave me good information. To sign a lease, I would need to pay rent for the first month, last month, and a security deposit.

Opening a store in a neighborhood like the Upper East Side of Manhattan would require me to part with $100,000—just to sign a lease.

With reminders from the lesson of Icarus, I understood that I would have to rethink my plan. Trying to emulate City Chemist would be the wrong decision, equivalent to Icarus trying to fly too high, too soon.

Renting a store in the wrong location would burn through my resources, and I would likely fall and crash. I needed to take a slower approach, working within my capabilities. Instead of going after something too big, I needed to lay out a more elaborate plan on how I could succeed given the resources I had.

After spending several hours on various websites to learn, I called the State Board of Pharmacy for New York. Fortunately, I found a helpful lady. When I told her that I wasn't able to find the information I needed about the state's requirements for pharmacies, she sent me a big packet of information with all of the details. I read every paragraph no less than 15 times. It gave me details that I needed.

For example, in New York, I could own a pharmacy as long as I hired a supervising pharmacist who would sign the pharmacy application with me.

The supervising pharmacist would be in charge of complying with all of the laws and regulations. The space itself would have to come with a certificate of occupancy that authorized me to use the space for a drug store.

The state required that I would need to have a minimum of 300 square feet, and reserve 100 square feet for the pharmacy area. I'd need to install a floor-to-ceiling wall to separate the pharmacy area from the general store. I'd have to install an alarm and motion detector to make sure that no one except authorized personnel could get into the pharmacy area.

The pharmacy area would need adequate heating and ventilation, with sufficient lighting, hot and cold water, refrigerators for storage of drugs and a thermometer. I'd have to have all of the right scales with weights and pharmaceutical equipment necessary to operate.

Clearly, before submitting my application, I'd have to invest a lot in construction—just to make sure the pharmacy was suitable.

If the pharmacy didn't make it, I wouldn't be able to get back any of the money I put into modifying the store. That meant I would need to be sure about what I was doing, and I would need to make sure that when I found the right store, the owner would have to agree to a long lease, at least five years with an option to renew the lease for another five years.

By doing all of that research, I was able to make better plans. The preliminary work of planning helped me realize that instead of renting a 5,000-square-foot megastore like City Chemist, I only needed 300 square feet at a minimum.

With a moderate-size store of about 1,000 square feet, I could likely succeed. I set a goal of paying between $3,000 and $4,000 in total monthly rent. As a small business, I felt that I'd always be able to sell enough goods to generate the money to pay rent of $3,000 to $4,000—but if I signed a lease that required more than $30,000 a month in rent, I would have too much pressure hanging over me.

If I hadn't done that research in advance, I could have gotten into real trouble. To someone who has not been in business before, $200,000 feels like a good nest egg. In retrospect, I can see how easily it would be to burn through that capital—before I even took in a single customer. Too many expenses would be like melting my wings! And if I made a single mistake at the start, I could have lost everything.

For example, if I would have signed a lease, gotten the store ready, and then submitted the application before I had the appropriate certificate of occupancy, the board would have rejected my application. I'd be stuck paying huge rent payments for years, without any income.

Some lawyers offered the service of preparing applications. But through my research, I learned that I could get through the entire process independently.

Lawyers would not have been able to advise me on all the details. When we make a commitment to succeed, we should not expect anyone to work harder for our success than we're willing to work ourselves. Although a lawyer could complete the paperwork for the state board of pharmacy, the lawyer would not know any of the details about running a successful pharmacy and making it succeed. Similarly, sitting in a classroom would not have taught what I learned from working and doing.

With years of experience, I felt as if I were the best qualified person to make decisions that would lead me forward.

———————

As a result of all I learned, other people hire me to help them make their pharmacies more successful—or to help them chart out a course to make better career choices. Like me, they realize that it doesn't make sense for some people to invest tens of thousands, or hundreds of thousands to attend a university if the person doesn't know what he or she wants to do.

A person could spend a fraction of that money to get real knowledge, like learning the art of *Greek Thinking*. We all learn from Plato's story about the prisoners in his Allegory of the Cave.

I had to stay organized, keeping my head in the game, completely.

With that mindset, I found the right location for my first store, at 77th Street and Third Avenue in Brooklyn. I named my store the Brooklyn Apothecary; I liked the Greek origins of the word.

In Greek, we spell apothecary φαρμακοποιός, ἀποθήκη, or *apothḗkē*, which means a storing place for medicine. When I approached the landlord, he agreed to work within my budget, and I signed a lease that would allow me to stay in the store for ten years.

I had to part with about $10,000, representing the rent for my first month, my last month, and a security deposit. It was the start of my investment and life as a small businessman.

When I signed that ten-year lease, I knew that I obligated myself fully, with a 100% commitment. I went all in, with my eyes wide open, and I intended to keep my head in the game fully.

The landlord provided me with the certificate of occupancy, showing that the building was zoned appropriately to operate a neighborhood pharmacy.

The previous tenant had operated the space as a nail salon, so the store would require extensive tenant improvements. To help me out, the landlord granted three months of free rent so that I could make the necessary revisions and work toward getting the appropriate licensing.

As a contractor, my dad helped to modify the store. With labor, shelving, and other equipment necessary to open, I invested more than $100,000 in addition to the rent.

I invested in the sign to advertise my store, awnings, painting, lighting, everything to build a family-friendly neighborhood store. None of those funds would come back to me, because the landlord owned the building. That's why it's called an investment—I invested in the dream of operating my own pharmacy.

Going back to the analogy from an earlier chapter, I planted my seed and spread the fertilizer. By nurturing the seed properly, I believed that seed would mature into a tree that would provide fruit for a lifetime.

The next investment included inventory, both medicines and sundry items to fill the shelves in the front of the store. By the time I went all in, I spent more than $160,000, leaving me with about $40,000 in the bank to get the store rolling.

Yet those funds wouldn't remain in the bank for long, because I had to hire a licensed supervising pharmacist to join me on the application. I would have to start paying for the pharmacist's time, even before the store started to generate any income.

Fortunately, over the years, I got to know many pharmacists. Understanding the importance of relationships, I kept in contact with them even when they moved on. After a few months of working together at City Chemist, one of the pharmacists that joined us, Nichole, fell in love and decided to move to California with her boyfriend.

Even though we didn't work together any longer, I kept in touch with Nichole after she left. In my mind, I always knew that keeping good relationships with people would be an asset. And keeping my relationship with Nichole helped out.

Coincidentally, around the same time that I worked to prepare my pharmacy, Nichole told me that she and her boyfriend had broken up and she would be returning to New York.

I offered her the position of working as the supervising pharmacist for the Brooklyn Apothecary. She agreed, and we prepared the paperwork together so that I could submit the application to the Board of Pharmacy.

All things considered, the process I followed led to a pretty smooth opening. I signed the lease in October of 2014. We finished the construction by November. And we submitted our application to the Board of Pharmacy before the holiday season of 2014 began.

In January of 2015, the New York Board of Pharmacy inspected our store. About two weeks later, the mail brought registration papers that authenticated the Brooklyn Apothecary as a licensed pharmacy.

Once we had the registration papers, I enrolled with the appropriate agencies to get my National Provider Identification number (NPI), my National Council for Prescription Drug Programs (NCPDP), and I registered the pharmacy with the Drug Enforcement Administration (DEA). With all four certifications, I could take the next step of registering with insurance companies.

Strategically, I didn't want to work with Medicare or Medicaid. Those government programs did a lot of good for society, but for a pharmacy owner, they came with complications.

With those programs, we'd get customers that wanted to fill prescriptions for controlled substances, like Oxycodone or OxyContin. For years, an opioid epidemic had been growing across the country.

People abused government programs to get their hands on those drugs, and they would always have a story. If we had to fill prescriptions for addicts, some of those addicts would sell the pills on the black market, then they would come back with a story about losing the pills and asking for more.

I wanted a good, clean, family-friendly pharmacy. Although many people needed Medicare or Medicaid, as a small, independently owned pharmacy, I had to weigh the benefits versus the risks. Medicare and Medicaid could open a larger consumer base in some markets, but those government insurance programs would bring additional risks. I would also have to pay a licensing fee to accept Medicare and Medicaid.

In my case, it just didn't make sense to work with government insurance programs. New business owners have to make their own decisions about the policies they're going to put into place.

Then, they needed to make a decision that would be best for them. They shouldn't base decisions on what anyone else was doing, or on what anyone else was telling them.

An experienced person could provide valuable advice, and we should listen—I listened and learned a great deal from the owners of City Chemist, and I'll always be grateful for their guidance. But at the end of the day, success comes to people who train their minds to make good business decisions that work for them, given their strengths and weaknesses.

Once I got all of my licenses in order, we were able to open the door to our first customers on my 30th birthday, February 26, 2016. I still remember our first sale.

A nice lady came in to buy a few greeting cards and candles. Those items proved to be great products to sell in the front of the store.

With only about 1,000 square feet of total space, I had to use all of my experience when considering what types of items to keep in the front of the store.

Rather than buying bulky products that took up a lot of shelf space, I packed the store with smaller products that had higher profit margins, and fast turnover. Scented candles, greeting cards, soaps, perfume, and cosmetics, turned out to be some of our best products.

Creating the Buzz:

While waiting for the insurance companies to approve us, I started getting ready to announce our store to the neighborhood. There are really two prongs to "keeping our head in the game."

The first prong is to make sure that we're aware of everything we need to know to build a successful venture. The second prong is to figure out steps we can take so that others become aware of us, and the value we provide.

As a new pharmacy, I had to think about the people in the neighborhood. They had a lot of options. Although I detested my competitors, the big, chain pharmacies. I didn't like them because I thought they destroyed the neighborhood culture.

As a Greek, I'm a big believer in building great relationships with the people around us. That mindset is what kept people like my grandmother growing stronger. For thousands of years, people in the Greek villages relied upon each other. By working together, helping each other, we built more fulfilling lives—at least that was how I saw the world.

I wanted to keep those traditions going. It's the way our parents raised us. With my sisters and brother, for example, my parents raised us in the traditional Greek way. T

hat meant we learned to think independently, and to always have respect for ourselves and for others. We may have grown up in America, but we are very much infused with the Greek culture of family and community. Now, our family is much larger. I have a total of 12 nephews and nieces—and I'll be using *Greek Thinking* to pass along our culture to them.

The big pharmacies didn't offer that kind of family-friendly service.

They didn't offer the personalized culture that the Brooklyn Apothecary would provide. I needed to let the customers know that we were different, that we would put them first, and not take advantage of them in the ways that I saw big pharmacies taking advantage of customers.

I had to send out the message that the Brooklyn Apothecary would be a different kind of neighborhood pharmacy, one that would respect people and serve their needs.

Since I didn't have an Internet presence and didn't have the time to learn how to use sophisticated marketing tools, I figured out other ways to connect with people.

I found a manufacturer that offered sundry items I could brand with my store's name. I settled on a package that would include 300 good-quality coffee mugs, scented candles, and gift bags, each with branding of our store.

After putting the gift bags together, with my personal business card in each bag that included my contact information, I started driving around the neighborhood. I'd knock on the door to introduce myself. If a person wasn't home, I left the bag on the door.

That strategy let people know that we were new in town and we were different. We would offer personalized service to people, helping them in ways that the big chains would not. It was a long-term strategy, not an overnight strategy. When people thought about the need for a pharmacy, I wanted them to think of the Brooklyn Apothecary as a friendly neighbor.

Again, remember the analogy of the seed. We don't plant a seed in the morning and expect to have a beautiful tree by the afternoon. We need to nurture that seed and feed the seed to help it grow. But once that seed grows into a tree, it can change our life.

If you want to change your life, think about the steps you can start taking now to grow:

» Step 1: Define Success,

» Step 2: Create the goals to take you from where you are to what you want to become,

» Step 3: Make your commitment,

» Step 4: If you fall off track, recalibrate with a vision of a better outcome,

» Step 5: Take incremental action steps,

» Step 6: Measure Progress,

» Step 7: Keep your head in the game.

» In the next chapter, we'll go over the next step—which is all about being authentic.

Being Authentic
Chapter 8

I've never been devoted to sports or athletics, but I remember hearing what a famous basketball coach said to inspire his team. As I recall, he said that everybody has the will to win. But having the will to win doesn't mean nearly as much as having *the will to prepare to win*.

If we're truly committed to reaching our highest potential, we've got to prepare. Ever since I returned from Miami, I felt as if I were preparing for a better life.

Each of the preparations put me on the pathway to exactly where I wanted to be. I'm facing challenges with the criminal justice system, and as I work through those challenges, I'm simultaneously thinking about what I learned along my journey:

» I'm thinking about lessons I learned from Socrates.

» I'm thinking about lessons I learned from other leaders.

» I'm thinking about lessons I learned while building my business.

In the first chapter of this book, I wrote about Socrates and his commitment to building stronger communities. When authorities charged him with wrongdoing, his friend Crito offered an opportunity to escape his punishment.

Socrates declined. Rather than running away from problems created by his decisions, Socrates chose to accept his punishment, knowing it would mean his certain death.

In a democracy, he said, a citizen has the right to work toward changing laws. A good citizen does not have the right to break laws that did not suit his needs. Instead of trying to escape his problems, Socrates worked to use his experience in ways that would help other people reach their highest potential. His courage and commitment have always inspired me.

We attribute Greece as being the birthplace of democracy. Leaders like Socrates, Plato, Aristotle, Epictetus, Hippocrates, Homer, and so many others helped to shape Western civilization as we know it.

Thanks to teaching from my parents and grandparents, those leaders also taught me how to think and grow and mature. Leaders taught me to live in the world as it exists, and not as I wanted it to be.

If the teachings of a man like Epictetus—a person who began his life as a slave—could last for thousands of years, I knew that we all could learn from hardship. If we're authentic, those leaders taught us, we can grow through hardship to happiness and fulfillment.

When I adhered to the values-based, goal-oriented strategies that leaders recommended, I prepared well and succeeded. When I did not, I brought challenges into my life, like when I ventured to South Florida, or like the decisions that put me in the challenges I'm facing today.

To overcome challenges, we need to prepare, and we need to be authentic. There's a recipe for authenticity in the same way that a recipe exists to make pharmaceutical medications. When we're truly striving to advance our life and become more successful, we follow a recipe:

» Step 1: We've got to define success

» Step 2: We've got to document the strategy that we're going to pursue

» Step 3: We've got to put priorities in place

» Step 4: We've got to develop tools, tactics, and resources to help us advance

» Step 5: We've got to measure our progress every day

This five-part recipe for authenticity has helped my family, it has helped me, and I'm confident that it will help anyone who wants to make real progress.

Leaders teach us that we can build better lives and better communities if we take a step-by-step approach. We focus on matters we control—and not on what others control.

That strategy got me out of debt, it helped me build a savings account, and it led to opening the Brooklyn Apothecary, which spawned other pharmacies, created jobs, and built stronger, more vibrant neighborhoods.

I'm using the same recipe for authenticity now, as I prepare to make it to the other side of my challenges with the criminal justice system. These words, sentences, and paragraphs you're reading make my commitment to building better communities self-evident.

I hope you've seen this commitment from the start of the book, and that you'll continue to see the commitment as we work through this ongoing project, including accompanying courses on personal development that I offer through my website, Greek-Thinking.com.

But first things first. Before I get into describing my experiences with the criminal justice system—and describing the strategies I'm using to overcome those challenges—let me show you what I learned from building a few neighborhood pharmacies. Ultimately, if I do my job well, readers should learn how they can deploy these strategies in their life.

All of us can learn from others; all of us can work to reach a higher potential.

Reaching our highest potential doesn't mean we're not going to have to go through some hurdles first. For example, when I opened the Brooklyn Apothecary, I made some principled decisions.

I wanted to build a family-friendly pharmacy. For that reason, I made the strategic decision that I would not accept government insurance—like Medicare or Medicaid.

My decision didn't imply that there was anything wrong with those groups.

It's just that government insurance did not fit within the type of business model that I wanted to build. Instead of interacting with the complications of government insurance companies, I wanted to work exclusively with private insurance companies.

As it turns out, although hundreds of insurance companies may advertise, four specific processors service those insurance companies. Those big processors include:

» OptumRx,

» CareMark,

» Express Scripts, and

» Humana.

To put it into perspective, the big insurance processors are like the big credit card companies—Visa, Mastercard, Discover, and American Express. We might have a Bloomingdale's credit card or an American Airlines credit card in our wallet, but those companies have relationships with the big credit card companies, and it's the credit card companies that process the charges.

Similarly, it's the big insurance processors that settle charges for the little insurance companies.

If the four big insurance processors agree to do business with a pharmacy, that means a pharmacy can basically serve any consumer that has private insurance. On the flip side, if a pharmacy doesn't have a relationship with those four big insurance processors, then the pharmacy would only be able to fill prescriptions for consumers who were paying cash for their medications—a very small market.

Once I received licenses from the Board of Pharmacy, and once I received authorizations from the National Provider Identification (NPI), the National Council for Prescription Drug Programs (NCPDP), and the Drug Enforcement Administration (DEA), I submitted my application to do business with each of the four insurance processors.

Challenges of working with a bureaucracy started—and they could be frustrating. Still, if we're authentic in our pursuit of success, we find our way.

When I reached out to OptumRx with hopes of getting approval to accept insurance, the officials scheduled March 7, 2016 as the day for my appointment. Since I opened the store on February 26, it wasn't too bad—only 10 days after I opened. I looked forward to the visit. But Optum sent its inspectors out early, without prior notice.

The inspectors inspected the store. Then I began the waiting process. Days passed. Weeks passed. No insurance. I didn't understand what happened.

Instead of giving up or allowing frustrations like I experienced with OptumRx to disrupt progress, we've got to keep going, pursuing our pathway to success.

Epictetus talked about how Stoic philosophy requires us to have the right mindset for success. We must distinguish those things that fall under our control from those things that we cannot control. We cannot get angry or upset by things that we cannot influence. Epictetus said:

> *Some things are in our control and others not. Things in our control are opinion, pursuit, desire, aversion, and, in a word, whatever are our own actions. Things not in our control are body, property, reputation, command, and in one word, what are not our own actions.*

I could not control decisions that people at OptumRx made. Certainly, the inspector could have told me his decision. Instead, he chose to leave me in the dark, waiting, wondering. He could see that I had invested my life into opening a pharmacy and offered guidance.

Instead, he chose not to communicate with me, leaving me wondering what was going on. Although my business meant everything to me, to him my business didn't mean anything.

I started to make inquiries. Finally, someone at OptumRx responded to my question, telling me that the inspectors did not give my pharmacy a passing score because I did not have a paper shredder on hand.

I didn't understand. The state and federal agencies had given me the authorizations I needed. I explained that I would go to an office supply store immediately to buy a paper shredder.

Sadly, the OptumRx representative said, I would have to go through a process, and the process may require me to wait as long as a full year before I could get a second inspection.

When I informed her that no one had told me anything about the need for a shredder, she seemed indifferent, citing policies and rules.

Being authentic means we create a process. We develop our own tools, tactics, and resources. Refusing to be imprisoned by a bureaucracy, I considered all of the other challenges I had to overcome. I remembered the strategy I used to help Richard Hunt, the customer of City Chemist who would have died in a hospital, alone, without family if I had not taken the initiative to find his brother, Charlie.

What did I do? I did the work! I started researching online to find a phone number, and I made the call. As a result of those efforts, Richard got to spend his final weeks in the company of his brother.

When I learned that OptumRx had rejected my application because I did not have a shredder, I shrugged off the inconvenience and went about my business. I first went to the office supply store to buy a shredder. Then I started doing my research, looking to see what I could learn about Optum-Rx.

Through extensive digging, I learned that Mark Thierer served as the Chief Executive Officer of the multi-billion-dollar insurance processor.

Then I took next steps, using every tool possible to connect. Although I didn't find him as quickly as I found Richard Hunt's brother, over time I found the home phone number of Mark. When we connected on the phone, I pleaded my case—explaining the problem I was having as a small, independent, neighborhood pharmacy. Even though he led a massive organization, I asked for his help.

Some may find it surprising, but when we're authentic and we ask for help, people listen. Mark agreed to intervene.

He took my contact information and connected me with the person at OptumRX that I needed to know. The next day, I got a phone call confirming that I would have a second inspection that week. And soon after I overcame the hurdle with OptumRX, each of the other insurance processors gave me the stamp of approval that Brooklyn Apothecary needed to begin filling prescriptions for consumers who had private insurance.

> *"Nothing great is created suddenly, any more than a bunch of grapes or a fig. If you tell me that you desire a fig, I answer you that there must be time. Let it first blossom, then bear fruit, then ripen."*
>
> —Epictetus

We all have to take our time and work through the challenges of our life. Sometimes we will face obstacles, yet we must work to overcome despite those obstacles. Leaders teach us that if we're authentic, we'll find our way.

Or, as Epictetus teaches:

———

"Demand not that events should happen as you wish; but wish them to happen as they do happen, and your life will be serene."

That's just another way of saying that we have to live in the world as it exists, and not as we want it to be.

With the massive buying power of big-chain pharmacies, I understood the possibility that they could be colluding to make it more difficult for the small, neighborhood pharmacies. I suspected that the big pharmacies could put pressure on suppliers, or possibly even on insurers.

Big pharmacies wanted to see small stores like Brooklyn Apothecary fail so that they could take advantage of customers without the customers even knowing it. They had their path and I had mine. They wanted to control the market, but I wanted to serve people.

My grievance against the big chains began long before, when I launched my own store. While I was a young man working at Argos Drugs, learning more about the trade, Mr. Dakis, the owner, taught me the importance of customer service, of making people at ease in the pharmacy. We had to be helpful.

Once I launched my own store, and I set my own pricing, I got even more insight into how large retailers took advantage of consumers.

For example, one nice lady responded to the packages I sent out in the neighborhood. She came into the Brooklyn Apothecary to thank me for the candle and coffee mug I left on her porch. As we spoke, she requested that I fill he

r prescription for a generic eye drop. She told me that she usually shopped at CVS, but after receiving my gift package, she wanted to learn more about what the Brooklyn Apothecary had to offer.

First and foremost, I told her that we cared, and we would service the community. As we chatted, I told her that the eye drop she requested would cost $70. Thinking that I had made a mistake, she asked me to check again. I didn't know whether she was telling me that I was charging too much or too little. When I told her the price was $70, she expressed disbelief, or shock. She told me that she had been paying the pharmacy at CVS $230 for the exact same medication.

"Why would you shop at CVS for your medications?" It never made sense to me why people would abandon the personalized service a neighborhood pharmacy could offer for the anonymity of a large chain pharmacy.

"Since they were bigger," she said, "I thought they would be less expensive."

Interactions with our neighbors brought customer loyalty to the Brooklyn Apothecary. They appreciated gestures like the gift packages I distributed two to three times a year.

If I ordered 300 gift packages, spending $10 each, I would invest $3,000 to build relationships.

Over the course of a month, I might distribute 10 of those packages each day, introducing myself to neighbors or leaving the packages on a person's porch. From those efforts, I might convert 10% of those people into loyal customers. That means 30 people would choose Brooklyn Apothecary over CVS.

If those 30 customers spent an average of $500 worth of medication over the course of a year, the effort would generate $15,000 in annual revenues for the store. That rather simple metric showed me that it made good sense to invest in building relationships.

More than earning a profit, I wanted to differentiate our store from the impersonal treatment of the big-chain stores. By listening and greeting every customer that came through our door, I built relationships. Those relationships led to a growing customer base.

Every customer became my friend, and every customer got my personal cell phone number. If they had a request, I encouraged them to call.

That strategy of following the recipe to authenticity worked both ways. By showing my loyalty to customers, the customers reciprocated, always striving to keep me in the know. Customers with whom I developed relationships wanted me to succeed, and if they suspected that something went wrong with the pharmacy, they would call to let me know.

It was as if they took pride in the neighborhood pharmacy—which was exactly what I wanted. That's what community is all about.

For example, recently, I received a phone call from a loyal customer. "Demetri," he said, "I've been coming to your store for a long time. You recently hired someone new and she reached out to me by text."

He sent me a screenshot of the message from his phone. She told the customer if he ran out of medicine, he should call her directly and she would give it to him on her own.

Had I not received that message from a loyal customer, I may never have known that an employee I hired was attempting to steal medication from the store and sell it directly to our customers. Theft may be a problem in any business, but a business with a strong community can lead to more opportunities.

Fortunately, the excellent service we provided led the store to perform well. In fact, as the store got going, I felt as if I were living my dream. With the intersection of hard work, dedication, happiness, and patience, I could get through the challenges. And we had our share in the beginning.

For one thing, when we opened the store, I only had about $40,000 in the bank. Sales brought resources in, but expenses sent resources out.

As the months passed after opening, I saw my bank balance fluctuate—and not in the direction I wanted. Instead of having $40,000 in the bank, my balance dropped to $30,000. Then to $20,000. Then to $14,000. Then it rose to $22,000. Then it dropped back to $13,000. Then it rose to $18,000. The challenges tested my nerves, but I remained true to the course, grateful for the decisions that I made, and happy to be living my dream. In time, the business picked up.

By my seventh month in business, everything started to click. The business began to sustain itself, leaving a little more in the bank than when I started. Without a doubt, the Brooklyn Apothecary became successful.

Eighteen months after starting the pharmacy, we were generating between $1,000 and $2,000 in sales every day. From those sales, I could hire seven people, which gave me a great sense of fulfillment.

The store did so well that I saved a sufficient sum to launch my second store, Village Pharmacy, at 150th and 12th avenue, in Whitestone, New York. And there is a great story with Village Pharmacy.

I began learning about the pharmacy business when I started with Argos Drugs. Mr. Dakis, the owner of Argos, was a kind man. After I moved on, we kind of lost touch. He had sold his store and went to work for another pharmacy.

Coincidentally, after I had signed the lease for the second store, I bumped into Mr. Dakis. At the time, I was in the midst of renovating the new store, getting it ready for licensing. As we reconnected, I told Mr. Dakis about my plans for Village Pharmacy and invited him to join me as the store's supervising pharmacist.

Mr. Dakis and I developed a perfect relationship. I had enormous respect for him, and I could count on his leadership to manage and run the store. The opportunity worked well for him, too, as he got to work in his neighborhood, where many customers knew, like, and trusted him.

Good planning and good luck allowed me to launch Village Pharmacy with the same recipe that had worked so well for me at the Brooklyn Apothecary. By relying on my own savings, I never had to feel the pressure that comes with bank debt or credit. After my learning experience in Florida, I wouldn't allow myself to fall into financial trouble again.

Some may wonder how a person gets lucky in building relationships with people like Mr. Dakis. In truth, luck is a tricky thing. As wise men tell us, luck isn't something that is fully in our control, but we can prepare to take advantage of luck if we make good decisions.

We can make ourselves luckier by following the recipe of authenticity. We have to put ourselves in a better position to help others, not just in a position to get more for ourselves. In being able to offer Mr. Dakis a position with Village Pharmacy, I got the greatest gift of all—to make someone's life better while I simultaneously made my life better. It was a double victory, and that is certainly good luck!

With leadership from Mr. Dakis, Village Pharmacy became equally successful. We provided jobs for seven more people.

Although I put a lot of hours into the business we were building, I never considered it work. The pharmacy became my life, my baby, bringing a sense of fulfillment and gratitude beyond my ability to describe.

Fewer than 18 months after the launch of Village Pharmacy, I had sufficient capital to follow the recipe again. I found a perfect storefront at the corner of 170th Street and Stanford, in Fresh Meadows.

After hiring a new pharmacist of record at the Brooklyn Apothecary, Nichole joined me to become the pharmacy of record at Stanford Pharmacy. We were at again, providing jobs and serving the local community.

———————

I opened the Brooklyn Apothecary on my birthday, in February of 2016. By 2017, I had Village Pharmacy operating. And in November of 2018, Stanford Pharmacy was operational. Some may wonder why I didn't call the pharmacies by a branded name. Like everything else, I made the decision strategically. I wanted to be a part of local communities.

A big, branded name never felt local to me. I am not saying it's bad. I have enormous respect for the leaders at City Chemist; they run an impressive, successful chain of seven pharmacies, all beautiful and in the best neighborhoods. Neighbors know, like, and trust them. But I build what is right for me, not what is right for other people.

Many people care too much about what other people think. They use the success of others to measure up and assess whether they're worthy.

As the Stoic philosophers write, "Ambition means tying your well-being to what other people say or do.

Self-indulgence means tying it to the things that happen to you." Real success, real mastery, or true authenticity comes only by tying our ambition to our own actions. All that really matters is the choices we make, the work we do, the judgment we use. As we become more successful, the less we care about external forces or what other people think.

When we stay on this path of authenticity, we advance prospects for further success. The harder we work, the luckier we become. When we deviate from this path of authenticity, we open Pandora's box, releasing unexpected problems into our life.

You saw that I deviated from that plan with my unplanned trip to Florida. Sadly, some disappointments led me astray from my principled path with my fourth store, which I'll describe in the next chapter.

In the story, we can see the salient message: At any time, we can veer off track. Our commitment to authenticity can let us recalibrate and start moving in the right direction again.

Follow the path of *Greek Thinking*, as we've been describing throughout:

» Step 1: Define Success,

» Step 2: Create the goals to take you from where you are to what you want to become,

» Step 3: Make your commitment,

» Step 4: If you fall off track, recalibrate with a vision of a better outcome,

» Step 5: Take incremental action steps,

» Step 6: Measure Progress,

» Step 7: Keep your head in the game,

» Step 8: Be authentic.

In the next chapter, we'll learn the importance of celebrating achievements.

Celebrating Achievements
Chapter 9

From my perspective, if a person wants to turn his or her life around, a four-part recipe will work. The previous chapters show each of those four parts in action—because just like millions of other people, I've had to turn my life around on several occasions, including now.

The first part to changing a person's life, is the person has to feel a sense of *disgust* with where he or she is at a given time. If we're disgusted, and the feeling is so unbearable that we truly want to change, we can push ourselves to take next steps.

As an example, I still remember sitting at that night-school desk, feeling disgusted with myself for being there. I may have been a teenager, but I knew I didn't like being in night school. My dad admonished me, telling me that if I didn't pay attention in regular school, I'd face all kinds of challenges.

When school administrators forced me to stay in a classroom with people that behaved more like criminals than students, the warnings my dad had given made a lot more sense. The other students were loud, aggressive, and clearly on a bad path. I felt disgusted with myself for being there.

The second clear example of me being disgusted was toward the end of the time that I spent in Florida. Up until I'd made that move, I felt strong and independent. I earned resources to buy my first car, I paid for it without taking out any debt.

I could cover costs for cross-country sightseeing trips I wanted to take before I graduated from high school. Foolishly, I then took a trip to Florida. Within a few months, all of my stability went down the drain. I not only burned through all of my savings, but I started to go into debt. Once I got so disgusted with myself that I couldn't take it anymore, I returned to New York.

When we're disgusted with where we are in life, we basically say *"I've had it!"* If anyone hates what they're doing, and truly wants a change, they may get to the point where they say *I've had it* and they may architect a plan to take the next step.

Disgust leads us to the second part in the recipe for making a change in our life. We've got to make different *decisions*. If we're disgusted, we've got to think about the decisions we made that put us in the position we're in.

We can't keep making the same decisions and think we're going to get a different result. That's crazy. If we know we made bad decisions in the past, and those bad decisions led us into a state of disgust, then the answer is simple: we've got to make different decisions!

The previous chapters show the different decisions I made after I reached my state of disgust.

To turn our life around, we follow the third stage in the process. That means we *desire* to live differently. That stage of desire is where we start to define success.

What is it that we want? If we know what we want, we can start laying out a plan to succeed. When the power of our desire for success grows stronger than "disgust" we feel for the stage of life we're in, we can start the real process of change.

In the fourth part, we *resolve* to make a difference. We lay out the plan with our goals, with our commitment, with our vision, with our actions. We hold ourselves accountable and take a step-by-step approach.

In living this way, we restore confidence and feel better about ourselves. We make a resolution that we will never revert to the type of behavior that could lead us down the bad path again.

Accepting this four-part recipe to change doesn't mean we won't make bad decisions in the future. We're human beings and we have flaws. That's okay. If we make a bad decision, however, we know that a recipe exists for us to recalibrate and get our life back on track.

It's the reason that no one has ever heard me express regret for the earlier choices I made that led to disgust with myself. That disgust prompted me to make a change. By making a change, I could get to the point where I celebrated incremental achievements.

In most cases, decisions we made along the way led to our disgust. Yet sometimes, external forces come into our life (like a pandemic) that can put us in a bad position. Either way, when we realize that we have the power within to make a change, we can start celebrating those small achievements we make along the way.

Even when we're climbing our way into a better life, we've got to give credit to the people that helped us grow. No one succeeds without help from others.

I've been blessed to have amazing teachers that spent time to help me along my path. My parents, my beloved grandmother, Greek thinkers and leaders all worked together to shape and influence my view of the world.

I learned to view everything through the lens of personal accountability. This view not only helped me to grow stronger, it helped me appreciate the influence that other people have had on my life along the way.

Some people want to take all the credit themselves, ignoring the fact that we're all a part of a broader community—that we're all connected.

In Greek mythology, we have the myth of Narcissus. Narcissus fell so much in love with his own beauty that he rejected everyone around him. He only wanted to love himself. If anyone tried to influence his life, he rejected them. His self-love became so overpowering that it killed him. When he saw his image in a pool of water, he bent down to kiss the beauty that he did not understand was a reflection of his own image. Narcissism killed him, as he fell into the pool of water and drowned—losing his life in the pursuit of his self-love.

We can't fall so much in love with ourselves that we don't recognize the contributions of all the people around us. To continue growing, we've got to celebrate more than our own achievements; we've also got to recognize the others that helped us overcome.

For example, when I set out to launch the Brooklyn Apothecary, I felt grateful to the supervising pharmacist that came to work with me, Nicole.

We had begun our friendship when she started working at City Chemist. Even though we only worked together for a few months before she moved to California, we stayed in touch. I felt grateful to her when she agreed to return and accept the role of being the supervising pharmacist for my first pharmacy. Being a petite, cheerful spirit that made everyone happy, I gave her the endearing nickname, Nicky.

When I started, I knew that I would work hard and strive to build more customer relationships. It had taken me about seven years to get out of debt and save the $200,000 necessary to launch my first store. Despite my not investing with City Chemist, I always felt grateful to the owners of that business for teaching me so much.

In the same way that working alongside Mr. Dakis taught me a great deal at Argos Drugs, the owners of City Chemist helped me to appreciate the importance of customer service and the pharmacy business.

It never occurred to me that within 18 months, the Brooklyn Apothecary would generate sufficient resources to return the entire $200,000 that I had invested to start the business. I couldn't have succeeded without the help I received along the way, especially from Nicky. As a result of our success, I had the resources to launch Village Pharmacy, and to reunite with my original mentor, Demetrius Dakis.

With two operating pharmacies, we were able to replenish the capital base again. I reinvested everything to launch the Stanford Pharmacy.

Again, I could count on Nicky to help me out. Jason Herber joined our team, accepting responsibilities as the supervising pharmacist for the Brooklyn Apothecary, while Nicky worked alongside me to get the Stanford Pharmacy up and running. Despite living in New Jersey, each workday she made the commute to make sure our pharmacy got ready for business.

Thanks to a great team, I had opportunities to celebrate achievements at many different stages. The success would not have been possible if it were not for people who willingly taught me about the pharmacy business, or with creditors that agreed to work with me so I could get out of debt, or with more than 20 people that agreed to build careers by taking jobs in the different pharmacies I owned.

Each incremental achievement helped me to contribute to building stronger neighborhoods, and I felt so grateful for relationships we built with the customers we served. We paid taxes that supported our school system, our police force, our fire department—all of which worked together to make society better for all.

Every opportunity I had to play a role in building a small business that helped to support neighborhoods made me feel as if I were worthy of the many blessings that had come my way.

As a first-generation American, I also felt as if I were giving hope to others. My father and mother immigrated to this country with only a dream. Through their efforts, they built businesses and provided my three sisters, my brother, and me with more opportunity. I didn't have a formal education, but because of the lessons I learned along the way, I became a small business owner. To show my appreciation, I wanted to help others reach their dreams.

With three stores going, our company built a really strong customer base. We would do anything to serve them. In some cases, I would travel overseas to deliver medicine that our customers wanted. There wasn't any distance I wouldn't go to show my appreciation for the people that trusted in us.

As a result, we built real loyalty from the people we served. And I wanted to repay the people that helped me to make it possible.

As our savings grew, I started looking for the next store that I would open. As I did when I took the job with City Chemist, I started by studying the train routes.

Knowing that Nicky had a tough commute from her home in New Jersey to the Stanford Pharmacy in Whitestone, I wanted to find a location where I could open a store that would ease Nicky's commute.

On the corner of Northern Boulevard and 164th street in Flushing, I spotted a vacant space that was only one block away from the train station near the Long Island Railroad. With a bank nearby, and a shipping center nearby, it would be perfect for our fourth store.

Although the space was bigger than any of our previous stores, the opportunity seemed like a logical next step. We had experience and a good track record. Further, I could use the fourth store as a central hub, using the new location to expand our business with online distribution.

I understood that many customers liked to shop on Amazon, and with four stores, we would have a lot of inventory. If we built an online presence, and we received too many orders, we could easily draw inventory from one of our other stores to fulfill the customer's order. Opening the fourth store would be the next logical step.

Wanting to show Nicole how much I appreciated her contributions to grow my business, I let her know that I would name the new store "Nicky's Pharmacy."

She deserved to celebrate the achievement of a fourth store, and this would be one way I could show her how much I appreciated her. She especially liked that the new store would ease her commute from home. Since she was engaged to be married, I also granted her a four-day workweek so she could take long weekends; I continued to pay her as if she worked a full week.

Nicky and I were united in our effort to continue growing. We wanted to provide an honest service that would help local residents. By opening more independent stores that operated in accordance with the principles we laid out, we intended to give real competition to the greedy stores that took advantage of customers. The high prices they charged, and the lack of service they provided, proved that they emphasized corporate profits over human relationships. I considered them greedy.

Pythagoras taught us a lesson about greed, showing how it eventually leads to emptiness.

Pythagoras was an Ionian Greek philosopher whose wisdom influenced Western Civilization over thousands of years.

His teachings influenced Plato, Aristotle, and millions of people since, including me. One of his inventions, known as the Pythagorean cup, teaches us what happens when we're too greedy. At first glass, a Pythagorean cup loo

ks normal—at least from the outside. On the inside, it has the shape of a Bundt pan, with a cylinder in the center. A hole exists beneath the center column, which connects to a pipe inside of the column.

Pythagoras designed the cup to help people understand the importance of moderation. By pouring a moderate amount of wine into the Pythagorean cup, it works fine.

If we're greedy with the wine, pouring too much into our cup, the wine would rise above the center column. If that happened, the cup would not allow us to drink at all. As soon as we tilted the cup to drink, if it had too much wine, the chamber in the center would drain all of the wine out from the hole in the bottom of the cup. We wouldn't get a single drop!

Pythagoras created that cup to teach us the importance of moderation in all things. Too much of anything is not good. But the big-chain pharmacies didn't seem to get this message.

Without exception, when I spoke with a new customer that visited one of our stores, we got a new loyal customer. They realized that we are a far better alternative, and I appreciated every opportunity to serve. With Nicky's pharmacy, I looked forward to bringing our consumer-friendly way of doing business to our home community in Flushing. We would always put people above profits.

Sadly, we faced challenges when opening the fourth store. When I faced those challenges, I got distracted again. Those distractions led me into a situation where, again, I'm having to recalibrate.

The distractions influenced a situation that led to my arrest. Now, I'm in a position where I must redeploy that four-part recipe of turning my life around that I described at the start of this chapter. Disgusted with where I am, I've had to make some new decisions. With a strong desire to get back on track, I'm resolved to make the change:

1. Disgust

2. Decisions

3. Desire

4. Resolve

Before I get into all of that, let me describe the challenges we faced when I tried to open Nicky's Pharmacy.

In November of 2019, we finished construction on the space. By then I had vast experience in laying out stores, and I felt really proud of the way we laid out the space.

We'd be able to make the highest and best use out of every square inch in the new store. We submitted our applications and got our approval right away from each of the state agencies—except for the DEA.

In my experience, the DEA approval only took a couple of days after the state board approved us. In this case, a few weeks passed, and we didn't hear anything.

I started to make inquiries. When I retained a lawyer to look into the matter, he told me that sometimes the DEA would do a spot check, and that could hold things up. Finally, in December, just before the Christmas holiday, we heard from the DEA. Two female agents scheduled an appointment to come inspect.

Nicole and I were waiting when the two agents from the DEA walked in for their inspection. I got a sense they were somewhat aggressive, almost rude in their questioning.

I didn't understand the posture they were taking. After all, they must have known that I'd been operating three other pharmacies without any incident.

When they asked if I had done a background check on Nicole, I confirmed that I had been doing a background check every month—as required by law. They asked to see the files I kept on background checks, which I provided right away.

Even though the agents acted like they were asking routine questions, the DEA ladies looked suspicious of something. Then they asked a direct question: "Who filled out the application?" Nicole acknowledged that she had filled out the application. "Why did you write that you'd never been arrested when you were arrested in November of 2014?"

I couldn't believe what I heard. I didn't know anything about Nicole having been arrested before. That arrest had never shown up on a background check.

"Did you lie," the DEA agent pressed her.

Nicole started to explain that it had been a misunderstanding. She had a disciplinary problem with the board of pharmacy, but the matter was resolved administratively. And as such, her lawyer told her that she would never have to answer that she'd been arrested before.

Nicole produced a document that showed the pharmacy board had resolved the matter—whatever it was—administratively, and there wasn't a criminal charge against her.

Then the DEA lady accused me of being negligent, because I had allowed the paperwork to go through without checking on the arrest. I objected to her tone, letting her know that I complied with all the rules and regulations.

Every month I did the background check, and I kept my files accurate, in order. If the state background reports did not show that she had an arrest, I didn't know how she could say I was negligent.

The DEA agents then left the store, saying that they had what they needed. They told me to watch for a questionnaire that would come in the mail, which would also describe next steps.

As soon as the ladies left, of course, Nicky started to cry. In all the years she'd worked with me, I'd never seen her cry before. I only knew her to be upbeat, positive, always optimistic. I understood the embarrassment she felt. Telling her she wasn't only an employee, but family, I gave her a hug. Wanting to comfort her, I assured Nicky that I would help her resolve this matter.

It would not have made sense to judge her. Every human being makes decisions that we'd like to forget or keep private. Since her lawyer told her she didn't have to report the incident, and the incident never showed up on a background check, I told her that I completely understood and that she had my support.

She offered to resign so I wouldn't have the problem. Although I could have accepted her resignation and hired another pharmacist, I promised to help her straighten everything out. Standing by her would be one way to show my loyalty. In our community, we don't leave the people we care about behind.

True to my word, I hired an attorney that would work to resolve matters for Nicky. While the weeks turned into months, I did my best to make the most of the situation. Without the DEA license, we weren't able to fulfill pharmaceutical prescriptions for customers.

While waiting, I studied everything I could about using the Amazon platform, and I began soliciting customers. Since I bought scented candles in bulk, I offered beautiful, scented candles by Voluspa and Nest.

Customers could purchase those candles from us at a lower price than they could buy from other vendors, but by the time we paid fees for packing, shipping, and the privilege of using the Amazon platform, the margins were quite low.

To make the venture work, I worked to cultivate relationships with customers that placed orders with us. Always with a strategy in mind, I hoped that customers would visit the online candle store I created, www.Oreanthe.com.

As the process dragged on, I continued to support Nicky. The lawyers did their best to assist her with the regulatory challenges she faced while they simultaneously worked to get our licensing in order. In the meantime, I launched an initiative to begin manufacturing my own brand of candles. In times of struggle, I truly felt that we could work together and overcome.

Sadly, in the midst of all those challenges, I discovered that my trust had been misplaced. While we worked together in the new store, I made the disappointing discovery that Nicole had betrayed our friendship by stealing.

I hoped she might provide some kind of plausible explanation. But the uncomfortable conversation that followed my discovery revealed more than I wanted to know. Rather than looking out for the store's interest, or treating me as family, Nicole violated the trust I had placed in her.

Despite the genuine fondness I felt for Nicole, we understood that it would be impossible for us to continue working together. She left the store that day, and in all honesty, my life began to implode.

Although I could have hired another supervising pharmacist to step into the role I had carved out for her, the loss of my friendship with her set me back. Taken together with challenges the DEA's investigation presented, I went into a tailspin of anger, and stopped making good decisions. We should never make decisions from a position of anger.

Emotions can cloud our good judgment, leading us into a disaster. It may have been a combination of working hard to manage three pharmacies while simultaneously trying to open a fourth store that led me into a rage. Either way, I failed to act in accordance with my character, and consequences followed that I deeply regret.

In life, we're given tasks and challenges. When we adhere to a disciplined path, we're able to overcome. As leaders have shown, with a disciplined path, we can overcome all challenges. Yet when we falter from the disciplined steps that we know can lead to success, we expose ourselves to setbacks, as I experienced after I parted ways with Nicole.

I made a reckless decision during a time of weakness, and as a result, federal authorities brought criminal charges against me. As of this writing, those charges remain unresolved.

Nevertheless, I face a new challenge that will require all of my intellect and discipline to overcome. Fortunately, leaders have taught me the path. As Hercules faced his labors with courage, I too will move through these tasks I face with my dignity intact, eager to continue as a law-abiding, contributing citizen.

I'll use the final chapter to show the plan I've laid out to prevail, regardless of what happens with the judicial proceedings ahead:

» Step 1: Define Success,

» Step 2: Create the goals to take you from where you are to what you want to become,

» Step 3: Make your commitment,

» Step 4: If you fall off track, recalibrate with a vision of a better outcome,

» Step 5: Take incremental action steps,

» Step 6: Measure Progress,

» Step 7: Keep your head in the game,

» Step 8: Be authentic,

» Step 9: Celebrate achievements.

In the next chapter, we'll see how adhering to this 10-step, disciplined strategy restores confidence, and can catapult us to the next phase of the journey. As I promised, I'll never ask anyone to do anything that I'm not doing. And through these lessons, I pray that readers will find hope to overcome challenges in their own life.

Expressing Gratitude
Chapter 10

As I write this final chapter of the manuscript, I'm watching the turmoil in Washington, DC with a heavy heart. On the one hand, I am sympathetic to the people who want to preserve their American rights.

On the other hand, I understand and respect the rule of law. Storming the Capitol in Washington DC has already brought dire consequences that those people did not intend. Five people have died.

Lengthy investigations and criminal prosecutions will follow. And all because emotions ran high and people lost their way.

The irony is that their futile effort to defend liberty and to support a law-and-order presidency will result in lengthy prison terms.

It's a Sophoclean tragedy!

Some people may wonder how a person who barely earned a high school diploma can advance to become the owner of a chain of pharmacies, and also be able to use such phrases as "Sophoclean tragedy."

The reason behind it all is Greek Thinking!

In America, and throughout Western Civilization, institutions of leadership rely upon the lessons we learned from the wisdom of ancient Greece. For example, in the architecture of Capitol buildings of every state—and the nation's Capitol—we see a tribute to the Parthenon, built on the Athenian Acropolis.

After more than 2,500 years, the Parthenon—built for democracy—remains a pillar of strength and inspiration for both leadership and higher learning.

I did not attend colleges or universities. But in most universities, students live in fraternities modeled after the Greeks—a culture that emphasized the importance of philosophy.

To the Stoics, philosophy wasn't only a way of thinking. It helped us to live better lives by giving us more insight into the human condition.

All institutions of higher learning strive to help students learn the lessons that have been passed down to me from my grandmother Oreanthe, from my parents, and from so many lessons I learned during my summer travels to Greece.

At some point over the years, I learned the story of Oedipus by Sophocles. The most famous of those stories, *Oedipus Rex*, or as we say in Greek, *oidípos týrannos*, shows how the decisions we make can change our life in a split second. Fate can sometimes overshadow our best efforts. The responsibility is ours to respond to our life reversals in the most positive ways possible.

Besides Homer, Sophocles may have been the most well-known of all the Greek poets. He wrote more than 120 plays, and those plays have survived for thousands of years. Why do the work of Greek poets and play-wrights live on?

Those artistic contributions to humanity live on because we see so much human truth in their stories. We know the Oedipus story, the Odysseus story, the Theseus story, the Narcissus story, the Daedalus story, and many others because Greek stories represent the fabric of human life.

Each of us has many layers, and we should never allow a single decision to be the determining factor on the complexity of our life. We see this through the wisdom of Plato's *Allegory of the Cave*, or Socrates' story of the *Crito*, or Aristotle's lessons on the importance of temperance and moderation.

There is always a backstory, always some context behind the decisions we make. And all of us can work toward making better decisions. The Greek wisdom helps us to appreciate what it truly means to be human, and with that appreciation comes more tolerance.

Within each of us we have wisdom, and we have foolishness. We
have strength, and we have weakness.
We have virtue, and we have vice. We
have goodness, and sadly, we have
traces of bad.

All of these conditions represent
a part of the human enigma, with different qualities coexisting within us.
We may be both cruel and kind. And
at any time, we can all work toward
becoming something better. In that
spirit, we can and should be tolerant
of others, even merciful in our judgment.

Although I may not have attended colleges or universities, the wisdom of Greece runs through my veins.
It has shaped my mind in many ways,
helping me to believe in myself, to
know that regardless of what's going
on around me, I must always work toward becoming better.

Greek Thinking helps me to live
in the world as it exists, and not as I
want it to be. From Stoic philosophers,
especially the teachings of Epictetus, I

learned that when I am down, I must revisit my principles and pick myself up. Indirectly, it was Epictetus who inspired me to write *Greek Thinking*, as I'll explain in the paragraphs that follow.

Impetuous Decisions:

Sadly, many of those people that stormed the capital on January 6, 2021 made a horrific decision, likely without much thinking about the consequences. There've been times when I made bad decisions without thinking of the consequences.

The pain that followed when that happened can be severe, even crippling, causing us to lose our way for a brief moment. It can happen to any of us. When it does, we must decide whether we're going to allow those aberrations to define us, or whether we're going to muster the strength to get back on track.

As I've written through the previous chapters, I lost my way with a trip to Florida. Rather than allowing that trip to define me, I used it as a lesson to grow.

And for a brief moment, in an effort to hold my business together, I made an impetuous decision that was totally out of character. Despite my intentions, accusations about an obstruction of justice led to my arrest and the challenges I currently face with the criminal justice system.

Since then, I've had to make a decision. How would I respond?

I refuse to allow a single problem with the criminal justice system to define me as a human being. In every person's life, I suspect there have been times that the person would like to forget. When my former employee, Nicky, learned that the DEA had discovered her prior arrest, I could see the horror of shame on her face. Instinctively, I embraced her, wanting to wipe away her humiliation. When we understand the wisdom of Homer and Plato and Sophocles, we live with empathy and compassion for others, knowing that anyone, at any time, can suffer a setback. For these reasons, we should temper or reserve our judgment of others.

The news media may advance their agenda with inflammatory stories about the people that protested in favor of President Trump. Yet I suspect that if we were to look closely at each person, we'd see that, like me, they are just people.

They are mothers and fathers, sisters and brothers, sons and daughters. They are people who work to contribute to the making of a better society, and they want to do the right thing. Sadly, in a single instant, they got carried away with emotions and passions about something they believed in. The explosive situation got out of hand, and events transpired that they did not intend.

Like everyone else, those people must deal with the consequences. We'd all be better off, however, if we learned to practice empathy in situations like these. Experience and the lessons I've learned have conditioned me to be harsh on myself, but more tolerant when it comes to judging the actions of others.

I suspect that in their hearts, those people see themselves as patriotic, law-abiding Americans. They want to see a strong country. They believe in the inalienable rights of liberty and all of what it means to be an American. In the heat of rhetoric— *which is another Greek term*—those people got carried away.

But it isn't the decisions they made in that moment that defines who they are as human beings. Like the rest of us, they have strengths and weaknesses.

Humans and Tragedy:

Aristotle defines rhetoric as "the faculty of over serving in any given case the available means of persuasion." Since victory in anything requires leaders to master rhetoric, Aristotle calls it "a combination of the science of logic and of the ethical branch of politics."

From Aristotle, we learn the importance of *logos, pathos*, and *ethos*. They are Greek terms that identify the tools of rhetoric that skilled speakers use to persuade. People skilled in rhetoric can whip their audience into a frenzy. Without discipline or restraint, in the heat of the moment emotions can overtake our logic.

Logos, or logic, provides us with a principled way of reasoning. *Pathos* makes an emotional appeal that, at times, can override our senses. And *Ethos,* or character, provides the guiding beliefs or ideals that characterize a community.

When a skillful orator like President Trump—whom I admire in many ways—invokes rhetoric and the wisdom of the Greeks, he can persuade people to get emotional, to lose their senses.

Although I don't agree with all of the "fake news" suggesting that the President wished ill on anyone, a tragedy occurred as a result of his rhetoric. For that, I am saddened, because it's clear that events of January 6 will tarnish his presidency, despite the good that I have seen him do for our country's economy.

As we read in the play of Sophocles, a human tragedy has unfolded.

Oedipus Rex is part of a trilogy that Sophocles wrote. Through three separate plays, including *Oedipus Rex, Oedipus at Colonus,* and *Antigone,* Sophocles takes us through the tragic life of Oedipus.

Oedipus had been the son of Laius and Jocasta, of the royal family of Thebes. When Laius was young, he committed a grave sin upon the family of another king. King Laius' wife, Jocasta, gave birth to their son, Oedipus. Wanting to know his son's future, Laius consulted with an Oracle. To his horror, the Oracle prophesied that Oedipus would grow up to kill his father and mate with his mother.

In an effort to protect his family, the King Laius hatched a plan to kill his infant son. He bound Oedipus' feet together and he ordered his wife, Jocasta, to kill their baby boy.

Unable to kill her own son, Jocasta handed the baby to a servant with an order to slay the infant. Rather than killing the baby, the servant left Oedipus on a mountaintop, where a shepherd rescued the baby. Later, the shepherd gave the boy to King Polybus and his wife Queen Merope, and they raised the infant Oedipus as their own son.

As he grew older, Oedipus heard a rumor that he was not the true son of Polybus. He asked the Delphic Oracle about his real parents. Instead of answering his question, the Oracle told Oedipus that he was destined to marry his mother and kill his father. Desperate to avoid his fate, Oedipus abandoned the household so as not to bring harm to the people he thought were his parents.

While on the road to Thebes, Oedipus encountered Laius, King of Thebes, whom he did not know was his true father. They began to fight over who had the right to pass.

When the old man moved to strike Oedipus, Oedipus threw the king down from his chariot, and the old man died. In that moment, Oedipus fulfilled the first part of the prophecy—killing his father.

The play continued with Oedipus performing a service for the people of Thebes; they rewarded him by giving him their queen, Jocasta. In mating with Jocasta, whom Oedipus did not know was his mother, Oedipus fulfilled the second part of the prophecy from the Oracle.

When they discovered the horror of their tragedy, Jocasta hung herself in shame. Likewise, Oedipus felt sickened by the knowledge that he had killed his father and slept with his mother. He gouged out his own eyes in despair, then walked through life as a blindman.

The Human Condition:

Sophocles tells the story much more eloquently than I have done here. Yet when I watch the civil unrest in Washington DC, I'm reminded of that terrible tragedy.

It shows that knowingly or unknowingly we all plant seeds through the course of our life. As we learned from earlier chapters, those seeds have to grow through a lot of shit to mature into the stories of our life.

Our responses to our struggles will always characterize who we are and what we become.

Last summer, thousands of people protested across the country. Like the gathering in DC on January 6, 2021, the people that gathered together in cities across America likely had reason to express their views.

Everyone has a First Amendment right in America; we all can express our views. Unfortunately, as human beings, we can make emotional decisions without thinking. When we get crazy with emotions, we make decisions that we would not ordinarily make.

The politics of passion can take over our life. Anyone can make a decision in a moment that we later regret. Some people can even get hurt. In the plays about Oedipus, Sophocles showed us that we all have a fate, and yet we all must make our decisions in how we respond.

In the aftermath of the summer protests, on July 26, 2020, President Trump signed an Executive Order to protect American monuments and combat "recent criminal violence."

That Order held that we needed a stronger law to punish people that attack our institutions. "My Administration will not allow violent mobs incited by a radical fringe to become the arbiters of the aspects of our history that can be celebrated in public spaces."

As a result of the Order President Trump signed, people who likely viewed themselves as protesting for liberty will now face 10 years in prison. Without a doubt, many of those will regret their decision.

The plays of Sophocles, however, do not suggest that the government will look kindly on them. Those people who thought that they were acting in the interest of liberty may be going to prison for a decade.

Lessons from Struggle:

As I watch the aftermath unfold from the disturbances in DC, I cannot help but reflect on the current Greek tragedy I've been living for the past several months. Despite the storybook journey of my career, I'm at a crossroads once again—a stage where I must recalibrate.

For several months, I've been living with this anxiety hanging over my head. Readers may be familiar with that cartoonish image of the Sword of Damocles, featuring a person strapped to a bed while a swinging sword keeps dropping down closer toward his neck. That's how I felt, wondering how my fate would unfold.

When I learned that authorities wanted to arrest me and charge me with a crime, I didn't understand. The crime, they alleged, related to obstruction of justice concerning a matter with the way that I responded to a government investigation. I didn't know how to react to the news.

The idea that a government agency would want to charge me with a crime really struck me as a tragedy. I went through the normal emotions, indignant that anyone would accuse me of a criminal action.

It just never occurred to me that people would see me as being anything other than a good person. From my perspective, everyone in society should view me as:

» A good American,

» A good Greek,

» A good son,

» A good brother,

» A good businessman, and

» A good employer.

But those charges against me suggested something entirely different. When authorities charge a person in federal court, the charging instrument starts off with: "The United States of America versus" the name of the person. I couldn't believe anyone would accuse me of a crime.

At that moment, I felt myself losing a little of the reason and sanity that characterized me as a human being—at least from my perspective. Those accusations took an emotional toll on me.

I had to come to terms with what the government had alleged, and I had to find the strength to adjust in a positive way. Although I had to live my fate, I did not want to be like the character in Sophocles' play, destroying myself because of a single bad decision.

I couldn't believe that a singular bad decision would be something I had to carry with me for the rest of my life. In a moment of recklessness, I responded emotionally rather than logically when I perceived an unnecessary intrusion of big-government regulators into my business. Their bureaucratic decisions threatened to obliterate all that I had worked to build. We simply wanted to open a lawful and legitimate business that would provide jobs and help to revive a local neighborhood in Flushing, Queens. But regulations slowed us down.

I wondered why we needed to have so many government regulations that interfered with business. It's one of the reasons I felt proud to support President Trump.

When he came into office, a wave of opportunity opened for people who wanted to work hard. Instead of stifling small business, his administration supported people who wanted to lift and improve their own lives. His business policies helped me advance from being a clerk to becoming a business owner. I could create jobs and play a small role in making life better for people in our community.

From my perspective, small business owners were the backbone of our economy. If we created more jobs, every person in the community would benefit. As I've heard financial analysts say before, "A rising tide lifts all ships." Good jobs result in more earnings. More earnings result in more tax revenues. More tax revenues result in more resources for schools, hospitals, law enforcement, and other social services.

As my business grew, and I employed more people, I had a good feeling. When I sensed that regulators were unnecessarily slow walking efforts I made to license Nicky's Pharmacy, my fourth store, I made a bad decision that I regret.

I wasn't trying to obstruct anything. Rather, I simply wanted to protect a business I loved. It was like my baby. I wanted to help the people who worked with me, and to serve the people that patronized our store. From my perspective, the government should have been helping me to build my business, not slowing down its growth.

Democracy:

As we come to the end of this story, however, we can return back to the lesson I offered at the beginning. It's the story of Socrates, a man of wisdom who helped me in so many ways.

In the first pages of this book, I wrote about an essential lesson that I learned from a story called *The Crito*, written by Socrates' student, Plato. In response to Crito's question about why Socrates would choose to suffer a sentence of execution, when instead he could leave, the answer Socrates gave changed my perspective:

We live in a democracy. In a democracy, we have to take the good with the bad. Athens has clothed me and fed me. It has educated me and protected me from foreign enemies. I have taken all of the good. I must also take the bad. And this is a bad law. But in a democracy, we have the right to work toward changing laws if we don't agree with those laws. We do not have the right to break laws.

Since I broke the law, I will pay the price for the bad decision I made. I will not run away like a coward from a problem that my own decisions created.

By reflecting on the teachings of Socrates, I turned my mind to other Stoic philosophers. They had shaped the way I lived my life. They taught me that regardless of what impossibilities we face, the burden is always on us to fight toward something better, to work toward a better outcome.

One of the Stoic philosophers, Marcus Aurelius, wrote how Epictetus influenced him. Aurelius grew up poor, living in an orphanage. Through the writings of Epictetus, Marcus Aurelius got inspired to make better decisions. He made a commitment to write his own book, a book he called *Meditations.*

In *Meditations*, Marcus Aurelius wrote down the lessons he learned from the leaders who lived before him, and he wrote the lessons he learned from the people who lived around him.

He learned to write about the good and the bad. Those writings helped him to understand that sometimes life goes our way, and sometimes it does not. Regardless of what's going on around us, however, we always must live in gratitude, appreciative of the journey we're on. We always must strive to do right, even after we may have done something wrong.

Marcus Aurelius wrote *Meditations* because he wanted to create a resource that would help him make better decisions. He read the book over and over, intending to use it as a tool that would help him respond better when fate worked against him. As a result of his writing, he rose to overcome the odds. Despite growing up through the struggle of living in an orphanage, he planted seeds and nurtured them. In time, he matured and grew in strength, eventually becoming one of the most powerful emperors in Western Civilization.

That story helped me to recalibrate and find my strength. Although I may not have written a book before, I knew that I had a duty and a responsibility to make things right. I could not change my fate, and I could not change my past decisions. What I could change would be how I responded, living in the world as it existed.

Like the Stoic philosophers, I could work to write down my experiences and pass along the wisdom others have passed along to me.

Some things are within our control, and some things are beyond our control. Yet with Greek Thinking, I'm confident each of us can find our way.

We must strive to be more like Odysseus than Oedipus, more willing to sail through the storms of life with dignity intact. Although we may lose our way in a given time, we do not need to gouge out our eyeballs if we face the challenges of our fate. Instead, we can face the impossibility with courage, and build our way to carve out the best possible outcome.

Additional Resources:

At any given time, a person may face challenges in life or business. Visit GreekThinking.com, where I offer mini courses and consulting services that others may use as a resource to reach a higher potential.

The one pledge I can make is that I'll never ask anyone to do anything that I'm not doing.

Made in the USA
Middletown, DE
02 February 2021